Illustrator:
Howard Chaney

Editor:
Janet Cain, M. Ed.

Editorial Project Manager:
Ina Massler Levin, M.A.

Editor in Chief:
Sharon Coan, M.S. Ed.

Art Director:
Elayne Roberts

Cover Artist:
Sue Fullam

Product Manager:
Phil Garcia

Imaging:
Alfred Lau

Publishers:
Rachelle Cracchiolo, M.S. Ed.
Mary Dupuy Smith, M.S. Ed.

How to Manage Your Multi-Age Classroom

Grades K-2

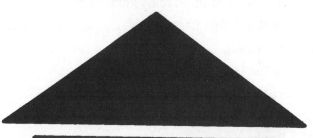

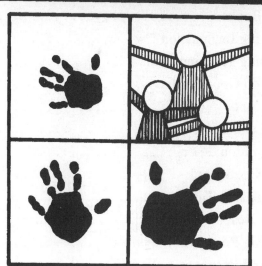

Author:

Sandra Merrick, M. Ed.

Teacher Created Materials, Inc.
P.O. Box 1040
Huntington Beach, CA 92647
ISBN-1-55734-468-X

©1996 Teacher Created Materials, Inc.   Made in U.S.A.

Table of Contents

Table of Contents (cont.)

Introduction

Purpose

The purpose of this book is to assist teachers who are working in multi-age classrooms. This includes teachers who are planning to begin multi-age assignments and those who have recently begun working in multi-age settings, as well as teachers who have been working in multi-age classrooms over the years. The emphasis is on classrooms that combine either first and second grades or kindergarten and first and second grades. Many of the suggestions will also work for K–3 combinations and 1–3 combinations.

Teachers Have Concerns

Many teachers face school reorganization with concern. Successful teachers worry that good methods will be discarded. New teachers wonder if they can handle the demands of a multi-age setting.

It is hoped this book will help teachers answer questions like these:

> *How do I teach two or more grade levels at the same time?*
>
> *What kinds of records do administrators want?*
>
> *Will the principal think my ability to manage behavior is poor if the classroom is noisy?*
>
> *Can students do well on tests without workbooks and worksheets?*

There is no single right answer to these questions; there are many right answers. Use the Table of Contents (pages 2–3) to look for topics, such as language arts, math, behavior management, and assessment, so that you can tackle your concerns one at a time. Choose one or two new strategies to try each week. Do not automatically abandon successful methods. You may choose to retain many of your own ideas if they produce good results. At the same time, be open to change. Some methods that sound unusual often produce excellent results.

New Ideas and Strategies

Although this book focuses on providing information about multi-age classrooms, it also touches on a variety of other ideas and strategies, such as those listed below. Some of these may be new to you.

- Whole language
- Integrated curriculum
- Cross-age tutoring
- Developmentally appropriate practices
- Portfolio assessment
- Center-based instruction

These innovations can and do exist outside the multi-age setting. Even though multi-age programs can begin without most of them, instruction in this type of classroom is most effective when these ideas and strategies are incorporated.

Understanding the Multi-Age Classroom

What Is a Multi-Age Classroom?

Games are everywhere, both the commercial kind and the educational variety. Learning centers and work stations are in the process of being renamed. Their new title may be blended curriculum environments. Developing specific instructional strategies and materials for multi-age classrooms should be a high priority. Some of this has already been accomplished with the application of whole language and integrated curriculum materials. There is an increasing emphasis on computers and technology just as there is in every other part of the world. Busy work is cut to a minimum or eliminated altogether.

Most multi-age classrooms focus on activities that are developmentally appropriate. Teachers who have not focused on these may need to refocus their thinking. Students age six through eight were expected to fit themselves to the school, rather than having the school accommodate the needs of the children. Multi-age classrooms feature learning centers, open time, sustained silent reading, varied room arrangements, cooperative learning, thematic learning, math manipulatives, and whole language tend to be child friendly.

Parents may not understand an unfamiliar type of education, and gaining their support will require the constant collective effort of teachers, administrators, and school boards. As teacher-parent communications and student reports evolve, every effort must be made to develop efficient, streamlined record keeping and reporting to prevent teachers from becoming overwhelmed by the paperwork.

Where Did Multi-Age Education Originate?

Multi-age education was very popular and widespread in the British Infant Schools almost thirty years ago. The English put their young children in large rooms combining five-, six-, and seven-year-olds. Their methods were those of a laboratory school. The rooms were full of projects, explorations, and experiments created by students and guided by teachers. By American standards these classrooms seemed extremely messy and noisy. In each class, the oldest children acted as tutors and leaders part of the time in an attempt to free the teacher so he or she could spend more time with individual students and carefully guide the small number of children who were just beginning to read. Children had an extreme amount of freedom. However, along with that, they also had an immense responsibility for their own learning.

Does Multi-Age Education Work?

Multi-age education does work. Today there are many adults in England who once attended multi-age classes who are now working at highly technical jobs. There are also thousands of people in the United States who were educated in multi-age classrooms. Branches of multi-age education have their roots in the United States as well as other parts of the world. (See The One Room Schoolhouse, page 7.)

Understanding the Multi-Age Classroom (cont.)

Overcoming Difficulties of Reorganization

Critics of non-graded programs are quick to point out difficulties. This is because graded programs have been used in some schools for 100 years or more. It would be naive to pretend that schools can be completely reorganized into non-graded classrooms in a few months or even a year. Teachers will need training to help them make a smooth transition from graded to non-graded programs. Ideally, teachers should attend college courses in multi-age education. Coursework should then be followed by practice teaching in both graded and multi-age classrooms. If college courses are not available, all staff development (in-service) days should focus on workshops concerning multi-age programs. The content of these workshops can include specifics on grading, classroom organization, grouping, instructional strategies, and behavior management. Many teachers may need more than a week or two of training to feel comfortable with the different facets of teaching in multi-age settings. It is easy to underestimate the time, cost, and preparation necessary for this type of reorganization.

Being Realistic About Preparation Needs

Time and preparation demands on the classroom teacher will be greater than those imposed by the traditional graded program. Outfitting each classroom with a wide range of teaching materials and manipulatives will be costlier than graded programs. More personnel, such as teachers' assistants, student teachers, or volunteers are usually required. Even experienced teachers will need more guidance, support, and administrative help, especially during the start-up phase. Some successful programs have a class size limit of 18 students per classroom.

Causes of Difficulty

Many problems can be avoided with careful planning and administrative support. Honest discussion can create a program that suits the unique needs of each school. A program that is very successful in one school may not meet the needs of another school. Multi-age programs are similar but not identical. For example some schools emphasize centers, while others do not have any centers.

The success of some multi-age programs may be the result of variables other than the multi-age component. When choosing a program to emulate, carefully investigate different settings and be sure to ask a large variety of questions. Does the school produce outstanding students no matter what instructional program is used? Does the program limit itself to a few volunteer or pre-selected students, creating an elite atmosphere? What kind of parental support/opposition does the program receive? Parents who want their children in these programs are usually very interested and highly involved in education. Is this the best program for your student population?

An open professional atmosphere where teachers feel free to ask questions, voice concerns, and even disagree will promote greater success. Educators should pick and choose specific aspects of each program to match the needs of their schools.

Old Ways Are New Again

The One Room Schoolhouse

Multi-age classrooms are not new in the United States. Many older adults once attended one room schoolhouses. These often served students from eight or more different grade levels in the same room. These small schools shared some of the philosophy of modern multi-age classrooms but not the physical room arrangement. Younger students learned a great deal by listening to the lessons of older students. Some students also served as tutors. All of the children had to take responsibility for their own learning since they spent most of the day working without the teacher's direction. They often presented their lessons by reciting aloud. The recitations were intended for the teacher, but the entire class benefited by hearing them.

Flexibility

Today's multi-age classrooms do not look like yesterday's traditional ones. They do not have rows of desks all facing the same direction. The rooms are filled with learning stations. There are tables and materials in every area. The furniture is moved around to facilitate different themes, seasons, and activities. For example, a large table may be part of the Home/Dramatic Play Center for housekeeping activities. It may then be moved to the Math Center for recording open-ended math projects, while the Home/Dramatic Play Center becomes a store. A visitor to a multi-age classroom should get the impression that this is a child-friendly setting, a room that invites students to explore and learn while having fun.

Noise Level

Not so many years ago, a noisy room was always considered to always be nonproductive and out of control. The opposite is now true. In today's classrooms, children are expected to talk to and learn from each other. With the use of learning centers, cooperative learning, and whole language, classrooms just became noisier as students worked. Teachers and administrators realized that students could not develop oral language skills by being quiet all day. Instead of seat work, children now read aloud to partners or practice reading aloud into a tape recorder. Sometimes they sing while reading a song chart in a learning center. A child may even sing or talk to a class pet. This is noise with a purpose. Active learning is developmentally appropriate, and it is very good for children. However, random off-task behavior is not tolerated because it is nonproductive and can lead to confusion.

Maria Montessori

Maria Montessori, born in 1870, was the first Italian woman to become a medical doctor. Her interest in education began while she was an intern in a psychiatric clinic in Rome. Retarded children were then housed in insane asylums. Her work with slow learning children led to a school for normal children called The Children's House (Casa dei Bambini) in the impoverished San Lorenzo section of Rome. Montessori attained amazing success. Many students in The Children's House learned to read, write, and do mathematics by age five or six.

The Children's House was multi-graded, with students from ages three to seven. They were taught with a variety of carefully sequenced materials that the students used as their abilities and interests dictated. Instruction was completely individualized. Each child progressed at his/her own rate. Older children served as models for younger ones. Instead of the teacher explaining the materials and activities to each child, students could learn by observing other students.

Montessori wrote about her successes in The Children's House in 1909. By 1913, her methods were the rage of Europe and America. There were about 200 authorized Montessori Schools in the United States by 1916. However, by 1918, interest in the Montessori method had diminished greatly in academic circles. When the space age began in the early 1960s, there was increasing concern for early childhood education. Around 1965, there was a rebirth of interest in Montessori's educational methods. As a result, Montessori schools were reintroduced in America.

It might be helpful for multi-age teachers to visit modern Montessori schools. Many such schools have made changes to incorporate the American view of education adding art and drama centers, reading stories, and encouraging language development. However, most Montessori schools usually retain the philosophy that children learn best while actively working with materials at their own pace, in a prepared environment. Since these programs can vary greatly, be sure to telephone each school before visiting. Make sure the school has five- and six-year-olds, since many are just preschools. Ask if there is multi-age grouping. In the traditional Montessori school, the child works alone or by observing other children. Even though there is little group interaction, mixing children of various ages provides a chance for older students to be leaders and instructors by example. Visiting a Montessori school can also provide a chance to see the interesting sequenced learning materials and to observe their self-teaching characteristics. If possible, arrange to see the presentation of a lesson. If there is not a school nearby, you may find it helpful to read Maria Montessori's book, *The Montessori Method* (Schocken Books, 1964), translated by Anne E. George, with an introduction by J. M. Hunt. The introduction is worth reading, too.

Making Preparations

Observing Other Programs

Schedule teacher field trips to other multi-age programs. It is important to visit several different schools so that you can compare. This works best if a group of teachers can go together to each site. On the trip home, you can discuss things you would like to incorporate into your own classrooms and also the things that concern you. Schedule follow-up meetings to make plans for your own program. It is essential that the principal visit some of the sites unless he/she has past experience with multi-age classes. Of course, take cameras and notebooks. You may wish to seek permission ahead of time to videotape the visit. Take the best from each and combine them to design classrooms and instruction to meet the needs of the students at your school.

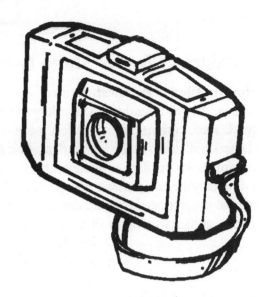

Doing Research

Ask the schools you visit to recommend books and articles that have been helpful to them. Read about the British Infant School and also multi-age programs here in America. See Professional Reading and Resources (page 144) for a list of suggested books. John Goodlad was one of the pioneers in non-graded schools. One of the most helpful books is *Transitions* by Regie Routman (Rigby & Heinemann, 1988). It includes lots of specific reading ideas that are useful for multi-age or graded classrooms. This is a good time to join the Internet and learn to use the information highway. Courses are offered by colleges, regional educational service centers, and some local districts. Although navigating the Internet can be difficult and frustrating to a beginner, new software is constantly being introduced to make the task easier. ERIC (Educational Research and Information Center) is usually the best source for educational information on the Internet. They provide a question answering service, as well. Ask for information on multi-age classrooms. You may be able to be more specific and ask for information on how to teach reading or math in the multi-age classroom. ERIC constantly adds new information.

Administrative Support

Setting up a multi-age classroom often involves radical changes. Such a program requires the enthusiastic support of the principal, curriculum coordinators, and the superintendent. Sometimes the school board must approve such restructuring. If necessary, work together to plan a presentation for the superintendent and the school board. Practice by presenting first to other teachers in a faculty meeting. Write down questions that arise in the practice session to ensure a smooth final presentation.

Parental Support

Hold meetings both during the day and at night for parents. Educating the parents about multi-age classes is one of the most important steps. To begin, invite parents to request that their children be included in the program. Encourage parents to ask questions. Provide sign-up forms at the meetings. Plan carefully for follow-up meetings; one meeting is not enough.

Characteristics of a Multi-Age Classroom

Combining Two or Three Grade Levels

The possible combinations are first and second grades, second and third grades, or third and fourth grades. If you intend to add kindergarten to first and second, do not add it until the second year. For a quick start, combine first and second in one classroom, and third and fourth in another. Place these classrooms side by side. A kindergarten classroom should also be nearby so that the five grade levels can function together as a mini-school. This involves going to lunch, physical education, music, art, and assemblies as a whole group. On Friday afternoons all grade levels combine in each classroom for special projects and presentations. Teachers of kindergarten, first-second, and third-fourth classrooms meet together weekly to share ideas and make plans.

Suggested Grade Combinations

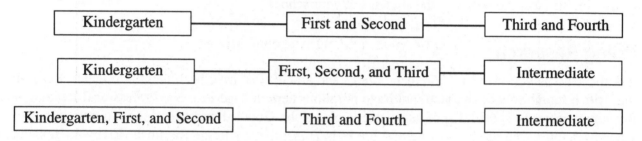

Kindergarten	First and Second	Third and Fourth
Kindergarten	First, Second, and Third	Intermediate
Kindergarten, First, and Second	Third and Fourth	Intermediate

Developmentally Appropriate Activities

A multi-age classroom is an active place. Children do not sit in rows of desks completing worksheets. Students spend much of their time working with real materials that foster discovery-type learning. Young children who are having difficulty with pencil and paper tasks are not forced to create products that are more appropriate for older children. Instead, they are expected to work with pegboards, clay, paint, puzzles, chalkboards, and markers to improve their fine motor skills. From these children, oral responses are considered just as important as written ones.

The teacher's evaluation is based on the child's ability to learn from the environment instead of a series of graded worksheets. Choosing activities that are "developmentally appropriate" means teaching to meet all the needs (intellectual, social, emotional, and physical) of the child. Learning takes place in a prepared environment with students working on projects in small groups. For a better understanding of developmentally appropriate practices see the sections in this book on Integrated Curriculum (page 14), Theme Centers (pages 76–87), Making Instruction Relevant (page 11), Continuous Progress (page 14), and Portfolio Assessment (pages 10, 125–130).

Portfolio Assessment

Arbitrary grades are no longer assigned. A portfolio allows teachers, administrators, parents, and peers to examine a broad sampling of each student's work. Emphasis is on progress and growth instead of a grade level standard. Anecdotal records are used to document achievement, including awards from sources such as art fairs, local contests, science fairs, and an interscholastic league.

Characteristics of a Multi-Age Classroom (cont.)

Thinking Skills

Multi-age classes emphasize the development of multi-dimensional skills that will prepare students for adulthood. Problem solving is at the top of the list, as opposed to rote memorization. This includes solving problems in all types of real-life situations, not just in math. Oral language skills have the same importance as written skills. Planning, organization, and self-evaluation are taught along with the three R's. Use of Bloom's Taxonomy (shown below) is encouraged, especially at the higher levels. Students are expected to analyze, create, evaluate, and make decisions. Lesson plans should reflect opportunities for problem solving, oral language, creativity, and analysis.

Bloom's Taxonomy

- **Knowledge:** Simple recall of details

- **Comprehension:** Understanding meaning

- **Application:** Extend learning to new situations

- **Analysis:** In-depth study of parts

- **Synthesis:** Create something new based on learning

- **Evaluation:** Appraise, critique, or judge

Emphasis on Process

In multi-age classes, knowing *how* to do something is just as important as taking a test or writing a composition. Vocabulary sequencing skills and real-life successes are enhanced by hands-on learning experiences. A variety of learning opportunities is necessary to produce well-rounded students. Good students know how to use many learning tools, including cameras, computers, microscopes, and art supplies. It is more important to know how to set up a scientific experiment than to recreate a perfect experiment. The ability to analyze mistakes is an important skill, since a great many scientific discoveries are the results of mistakes. A truly educated person should be able to analyze unexpected results and draw insightful conclusions, since this process is a source of new knowledge.

Making Instruction Relevant

The use of experts from the real world, as resource persons, is emphasized. Some examples include: a music demonstration given by a guitar teacher, a presentation and display given by a person whose hobby is collecting Native American artifacts, a display shown by a woman whose farm yielded many museum-quality fossils. Numerous field trips to ordinary places like printing shops and post offices are encouraged. Of course, it is also important to visit historical sites, museums, and zoos. Care should be taken to choose instructional materials that reflect real-life problems and situations, the genuine interests of children.

Characteristics of a Multi-Age Classroom (cont.)

Guided Choices

Each day students make choices about what center to visit, what materials to use, which books to read, and how to present their projects. In some multi-age classrooms there are no assigned activities in the learning centers. This gives children the freedom to explore their interests and individual learning styles. With this freedom comes the responsibility to discuss and explain the chosen activity or the created product. This helps children to grow into adults who know how to make decisions. This does not mean that teachers cannot assign work to be done. Student choices can be limited. Constant teacher observation and feedback assures that students learn how to make choices.

Whole Language

Children learn to read in the same way that they learn to talk, by repeated exposure to words. It is better to reward approximations than to emphasize and grade mistakes. This does not mean that phonics and reading skills are not taught. They are integrated into interesting reading materials in a meaningful way. Students do not have to read specific material but may choose books that suit their interests as well as reading level. However, it may be necessary to limit choices to increase the chances for student success. For a more complete description of whole language, see page 31.

Characteristics of a Multi-Age Classroom (cont.)

Parental Involvement

In the first year, it is vital to get the parents involved. Do not assume that just attending a meeting and signing up for a new program will ensure parental support. Inviting parents to visit the classroom and attend presentations is extremely important.

Every effort should be made to enlist supportive attitudes from parents through classroom visitations. Make a big push to get parents to visit the classroom at least once. Parents will feel more comfortable if they are busy, so plan a simple activity for them to do with their children, especially on the first visit. Teachers should also encourage parents to come on a regular basis to act as teaching assistants. Parents who have worked in the classroom are less likely to become dissatisfied with the multi-age structure.

A high level of communication is maintained between home and school. Frequent notes and newsletters also help build a strong bond. Remember that you have to keep the faith of these parents in the multi-age program for two to four years.

Parents are invited to visit the school for parent nights at least twice a year. A parent night for a multi-age school is organized like an open house, but the activities can be more specific. Usually there is one parent night in the fall and one in the spring. After visiting the classroom, parents can be directed to special talks located in other rooms such as the computer lab, library, and cafetorium. Presenters might include personnel such as the reading specialist, who can describe whole language and invented spelling; support teachers, who might tell about the use of computers; and the assistant principal, who can explain authentic assessment and the curriculum.

These talks should begin every thirty minutes and last about twenty minutes. Since every school is different, the presenters, topics, and locations should be tailored to meet the needs of your school. In addition to discussing multi-age classes, you may wish to tell about recent changes in education. Parents need answers but are not sure what questions to ask. Bulletin boards in the halls and classrooms can convey specific information. See pages 10–12 and 14 to get some ideas for displays and presentation topics. Handouts enhance classroom visits and presentations.

Parent nights are still a good time to discuss the child's portfolio with the parent and/or child. Together you can decide which pieces to send home and which should go into the portfolio. Reviewing, evaluating, and choosing materials for a child's portfolio is part of his/her parents' responsibility. If more time is needed, parents can sign up for conferences. Have a sign-up sheet available for this purpose. Reproduce the Conference Sign-Up Sheet (page 15) or create one of your own. You may wish to fill in the dates and times you have available before asking parents to sign up for conferences. This should prevent them from requesting conferences during class time or when you have other commitments, such as meetings and workshops. Use the Parent-Teacher Conference Form (page 132) to document the information that you share with the parents.

Conference Sign-Up Sheet

Date	Time	Parent's Name	Student's Name	Telephone Number

Characteristics of a Multi-Age Classroom (cont.)

Continuous Progress

Every effort is made to match the learner to developmentally appropriate tasks. A student who has not learned to count is not expected to add and subtract. Some students may read on a second grade level and do math on a first grade level. Children with special interests or abilities in a particular areas, such as art or music, may work with older students. Since children work at their own rate, retention is never considered. Students who did not master all the objectives traditionally done in the first grade will not be required to do all the first grade work over again. They will begin the next year at the point at which they stopped the year before. Continuous progress requires a high level of individualization.

Integrated Curriculum

Real life is not divided into separate subject areas. Teachers of multi-age classrooms rely on thematic units to extend learning across the curriculum. By using a theme, a teacher can plan activities throughout the day that lead to a cohesive, in-depth study of the topic. Students will be practicing and applying their skills in meaningful contexts. Consequently, they will tend to learn and retain more. Both teachers and students will be freed from a day that is broken into unrelated segments of isolated drill and practice. For a full explanation of using themes in the classroom, see pages 76–87.

Flexible Grouping

Groups may meet for a variety of purposes with and without the teacher. Grouping may be based on interests, learning needs, cooperative learning, etc. Students often help one another and work in mixed-age groups. For example, students in one science project group may be preparing books on clouds. The topic is the same for all of the students in that group, but the teacher will have different expectations about the level of the finished products, depending on each student's age. Flexible groups are sometimes smaller than traditional reading groups and change membership as student needs and interests change. For more information about how to use flexible grouping, see pages 21–22.

Modeling

One important feature of multi-age classrooms occurs with little effort on the part of the teacher. If older students and younger students are in close proximity while engaging in learning activities, the younger students will seek to imitate the behaviors modeled by the older students. This type of learning is often observed in homes when a younger sibling watches his/her older brother or sister use a computer and then suddenly demonstrates advanced computer knowledge. Some children have come into kindergarten already knowing how to read because they played school with older siblings. Direct tutoring by the older child is not required. It is only necessary to model the desired behavior or play school with the younger child. Nothing is more interesting to a child than another child who has the skills that he or she wants to acquire.

Conference Sign-Up Sheet

Date	Time	Parent's Name	Student's Name	Telephone Number

Kindergarten in a Multi-Age System

Kindergarten as a Separate Entity

Some multi-age schools do not include kindergarten in the mix. The reason for this separation is usually because it avoids combining readers with non-readers. Even if kindergartners are able to read, their developmental level and lack of fine motor skills make concrete experiences more appropriate than pencil and paper tasks. For young children, the emphasis is on process, not product. Kindergarten as a separate year can be a good preparation for multi-age classes. Students learn to be self-starters, working in centers. They begin to make choices about what and how to learn. Their responses to the learning environment and to literature can and must be freer than those of older children. Sometimes kindergarten is located in a special kindergarten center or early childhood center. At other times, kindergarten classes are part of an elementary school but are not included in the mixed-age settings that have been set up on that campus.

Partial Joining of Kindergarten

If kindergarten is located on the same campus as the other primary grades, there can be a partial joining during the day without losing the special nature of kindergarten. Young students join with older students for selected activities such as physical education, music, art, lunch, recess, field trips, assemblies, festivals, and performances. Sometimes different ages are mixed for special social studies or science presentations on a once-a-week basis. Each kindergarten class is partnered, by assignment or choice, with a specific first and second grade mixed-age class. The mixed-age class is usually the one that the kindergartners will attend when they enter first grade. This enables students to develop on-going friendships that continue year after year. Kindergarten students can form relationships with the older students before joining them on a full-time basis. This arrangement also provides opportunities for them to get acquainted with the mixed-age teacher whom they will have for the next two years.

Mixed-Age Primary

Another possibility is to create a mixed-age class that combines kindergarten and first and second grades. This arrangement is successful in many classrooms. In some cases, visitors are so impressed by the capabilities, self-assurance, and self-discipline of all the children that they have to ask which students are the kindergartners. Watching the older children perform tasks seems to help the kindergartners mature at a faster rate and promote a positive self-concept. This type of mixed-age class usually has 7–8 kindergartners, 7–8 first graders, and 7–8 second graders. There are some obvious advantages to this type of structure. The oldest students become little assistant teachers to model and explain things to the younger children when they need help. Rather than having a classroom full of children who are just beginning to read, there are only 7–8 students who are at this stage. Students making their first attempts at reading require extra time and intensive instruction from the teacher. It is usually easier to do this for eight students than for twenty or more pupils as in traditional graded classes.

Kindergarten in a Multi-Age System (cont.)

Teaching Readers and Non-Readers Together

The addition of non-readers (kindergartners) to readers (first, second, and sometimes third graders) is made easier by changes in the physical environment of primary classrooms. Younger children adapt better when allowed to engage in active learning and given more time in learning centers. However, success depends on many factors. Preparation of the classroom, the teacher's ability, and individual student differences all play a role. In some instances, problems might arise if the teacher has not received enough training or does not have adequate materials for center-based education. It is also possible that if most of the kindergarten students were especially noisy, extremely active, or very immature, the learning process might be disrupted for the older students. Many schools are seeking to prevent such an occurrence by providing pre-school classes for children who might not otherwise be well prepared for school. Classes are often available for three- and four-year-olds, and some schools have training that begins at birth.

Different Settings for Kindergartners in Multi-Age Classes

Some classes have kindergartners staying all day, just like the older children. This presents something of a problem for the children who still take naps. It is usually resolved by teachers working in pairs. One teacher stays with the napping students in his or her classroom, while the other teacher allows the rest of the children to have free choice of center play. This is not a perfect solution because it sometimes causes crowding. Some schools try to avoid this problem by limiting class size to about 18 students. Many of the model multi-age schools also provide a classroom assistant for at least half of the school day.

In another multi-age program, the kindergartners attend school for half a day. They go home at lunchtime, and the teacher has the help of the assistant during the morning. The assistant is often responsible for the small group lesson presented to the kindergartners. This arrangement allows the teacher to provide lots of individual attention, especially for beginning readers. In some cases, there are only 12 students in the class after lunch. With this low pupil-to-teacher ratio, the teacher can do one-to-one instruction, the most effective method of teaching.

In other K–2 and K–3 classes, the kindergartners go half days in the fall and switch to whole days in late winter or early spring. Those children still needing a nap might not start all-day programs until the next year. Some children who are very young or very immature might also wait until the following year to begin staying all day. Each child is evaluated on an individual basis.

Which to Choose?

All of these arrangements work well if they are tailored to fit individual schools. What works well for one school may not work well for another. For example, a committee visits a program that works extremely well because there are only 18 students in each classroom. If this same model is used with 22 or 25 students per classroom, it may not work.

Models of Multi-Age Classrooms

Model 1

This model functions almost like a traditional classroom. The underlying structure is that of reading groups (ability grouped) for most of the morning, while the other groups do seat work (worksheets) at tables in centers. Although the students are seated at the centers, they do not use any of the manipulatives during the morning. The classroom serves kindergarten and first and second graders. All grades are seated together in a mixed fashion. In each center, there are students from every grade level. However, the work is assigned based on each child's current grade-level placement. In other words, the kindergarten children are doing kindergarten worksheets, the first graders are doing first-grade worksheets, and the second graders are doing second-grade worksheets. A few children in the Listening Center are singing a song and pointing to a music chart, and a few in the Science Center are holding animals, observing them, and having a discussion.

Although the morning activities are much like any traditional classroom, it is immediately obvious to visitors that this is a multi-age classroom. There is a high noise level in the room. Sometimes the teacher has trouble hearing the children who are reading aloud to her. The two groups in the Science and Listening Centers are laughing and singing happily. In the traditional classroom, this would be considered misbehavior even though the children are on task. The children working on the worksheets are eating a snack related to the class theme. They are smiling and talking softly. Older children are answering questions about the younger children's worksheets. All of the older children serve as occasional tutors

so the teacher's reading group will not be interrupted. Music related to the class theme is playing softly in another corner of the room. In one center there is an extensive display of objects related to the theme; most of them were brought by the children. In the afternoon most of the kindergarten children snack and sleep, while the older children work freely with all of the materials in the centers.

Special parent reports are used instead of report cards. In the first year of multi-age teaching, teachers at this school tried to use a variety of checklists for grading purposes. However, this has been largely abandoned because teachers were spending all of their time testing objectives instead of teaching them.

This is an example of a transitional classroom where the teacher is slowly moving from traditional classroom practices to a multi-age structure. It may take several years for all the characteristics of a multi-age classroom to appear. In the meantime, the children are definitely learning and appear to be enjoying school. The teacher is confident that she is covering all the objectives required. She has been teaching in a multi-age classroom for several years. Parents are very involved in the day-to-day activities of the classroom. They meet once a month with the teacher to make activities for the centers and often come to volunteer. Many of the decorations displayed in the classroom are done by parents.

Models of Multi-Age Classrooms (cont.)

Model 2

The teacher has five reading groups, all ability grouped. The class has first and second graders but no kindergartners. The classroom is arranged in work stations and is very quiet except for low work noise. The teacher uses a very soft, slow speaking voice, which is imitated by the children. All of the children are smiling and busy. Most of the morning and part of the afternoon are spent on reading activities. The teacher works with two reading groups in the morning and one in the afternoon. She also tours the tables and work stations to do some on-the-spot conferencing, make notes, and listen to some oral reading. Children in the group for beginning readers are worked with every day. The other reading groups are seen every other day. Reading groups use whole language readers, trade books, and traditional textbooks which are teacher chosen.

Most of the children in the centers are not doing worksheets. Some are working on projects of their own choosing, while others are doing projects assigned by the teacher. Early in the year, center rotation is assigned by the teacher. Later, children are allowed to sign up for centers each morning. All of the centers are designed to be very quiet. Music and tapes are all listened to with headphones, and there is no loud singing or background music. There are no animals in the classroom, and the Science Center consists of a small rock and leaf exhibit. Only a few children are doing worksheets, and most of these are research projects, math measurement activities, or tests. During most of the afternoon in this classroom, there are math and science lessons similar to those in more traditional classrooms. There are formal art lessons. Children do not have daily access to art materials but use them at appointed times. Some afternoons are spent in a math laboratory setting, and the teacher plans to do more hands-on math centers next year.

There are many examples of student-created books displayed around the room. The centers in the room are for writing, listening, research, math, library, and science. Authors are featured in the Listening Center. There are tables in the Writing Center and in the Math Center and some multi-purpose tables in the middle of the classroom. Even though there is a specific Library Center, most of the books are on shelves near the teacher's desk. There are hundreds of them!

This teacher is completing her first year in a multi-age classroom. Most of her time this year is being spent redesigning her reading program and learning to manage five reading groups. This teacher does a great deal of record keeping. There is always a small notebook or a clipboard in her hand, and she frequently observes the children to assess their progress. The teachers at this school recently redesigned their report cards so that they would be more informative for parents.

In addition, there are many long checklists to be marked. Portfolios of children's work are kept. After school, the teacher spends most afternoons completing records. The fact that there are only a few worksheets being used in this classroom indicates that the teacher spends additional time planning special activities.

Models of Multi-Age Classrooms (cont.)

Model 3

This classroom has a functional room arrangement with many materials and lots of furniture. The classroom is full of centers. There is only a small rug area by the chalkboard for whole-class gatherings. This particular room is a little crowded because it is in a very old building with average classroom space. These classrooms were designed to house rows of desks, a teacher desk, and a reading table. A great deal of time has been spent on room planning and stocking centers. It is immediately apparent that there are many center-based activities available for the students. There is an Art Center with three large easels providing places for six children to paint. The Math Center has two low shelves chock full of manipulatives, and two small tables are pushed together between the shelves. There is a Game and Activity Center containing a variety of manipulatives. However, the children in this center are working together on a worksheet. They have cut apart a word on the worksheet and are trying to write down as many new words they can make from the original word. It is a mixed group of kindergartners and first and second graders. Children in the Math Center are measuring the tables with cubes in order to fill in the blanks on a worksheet. Students in the Science Center are making books about clouds. Most of the materials have been prepared in advance, and the exact type of book to be made was assigned by the teacher. There are several library books about clouds on a nearby shelf. Near the teacher is a Skills Center filled with several boxes of worksheets and folders that are color coded for each grade level. The library books are in this center, too. There is a tiny Listening Center near the door with a box of books and tapes. Near the classroom rug is a long shelf with cubbyholes full of math manipulatives in tubs and buckets. This shelf and an additional Math Center are used for an hour or more each afternoon to do activities from Mary Baratta-Lorton's *Mathematics Their Way* (Addison-Wesley, 1993). During the morning, the teacher calls small groups, some are ability grouped, or individuals to the rug area for reading and spelling. No one is painting in the Art Center. However, a few children are nearby, coloring a worksheet. It is impossible for visitors to identify the kindergarten children since they all seem to be doing above- average work. The room is quiet for so much activity to be taking place, and the kindergarten children behave as well as the first and second graders.

This teacher has several years of experience in multi-age classrooms. Her emphasis is on center design. She spends her time after school planning the activities for each grade level so that there are three sets of everything. The room is very neat, and the centers seem almost unused. The Math Center and the Listening Center seem to get more use than the other centers. The teacher is making plans to use the centers for more student activities next year even though there will be an increase in the noise level. She is beginning to let the students participate more in the planning stages of instruction.

Flexible Grouping

Flexible grouping simply means that children no longer spend the morning ability grouped with children of the same age. A few years ago every teacher was expected to have three reading groups assigned by ability. Now teachers may group for reasons other than ability, such as social skills or children's interests. Some teachers do little or no grouping during the language arts period. However, flexible grouping may occur during math and other subjects in the multi-age classroom. The main focus of this type of setting is to provide individualization for each student.

Flexible Grouping for Centers

Students are not assigned to centers by age or ability. When the year begins, the teacher carefully creates mixed groups of students. The ability of the group to work together in a friendly manner is of utmost importance. Oddly enough, cooperation is enhanced by the greatest mix. It seems to produce less competition. In each group, there should be one older child who can give assistance and answer simple questions. There should also be at least one of the youngest children in each group. Very active students who are weak in social skills should be separated from each other and placed in different groups. In the first few weeks, the focus is on having students stay on task while helping each other. Refer to some of your teacher resource books for cooperative learning activities. With this type of beginning, discipline problems are greatly reduced and are often eliminated during center time. Note that this grouping is already flexible in that it is the complete opposite of ability and age grouping. Social skills come first, followed by cooperative learning.

Later in the year more flexibility and freedom can be added by allowing choice in the centers. The primary concern is for having students learn responsibility. In every part of life, responsibility is the prerequisite of freedom. At first, children may be allowed to sign up for centers only one day each week. Once free choice is in operation, teachers may stipulate that time in each center be limited to one day. Those students wishing to spend two days in the same center to finish a product may state their case to the teacher during sign-up time. The teacher can step in at any time to impose limits, make suggestions, change students to another center, etc. Repeated visits to the same center by the same student may or may not be desirable, and action should be taken on an individual basis. For example, boys wanting to build with blocks every day should be asked to sign up for all the other centers before returning to the blocks. However, a child struggling toward success who has become involved and productive in a center should be allowed to return to that center as often as possible. In some instances, it may be midyear before full choice in centers is allowed. In others, it may be five or six weeks. Once free choice is an option, students may sign up for a center two days in a row before changing to a new center. If students object, the teacher should suggest an extension activity in another center. Girls wanting to play with dolls in the house every day can be encouraged to paint a picture of their favorite dolls, write a story about the dolls, design a house or furniture for the dolls, read doll stories, research dolls from long ago, or create craft dolls in the Art Center. The teacher checks the sign-up sheet every day for problems and hold individual conferences about discipline and procedures as necessary.

Flexible Grouping (cont.)

Partners

Partners are also a type of flexible grouping and serve many purposes in the classroom. Partners may be any combination of ages, abilities, or sexes. One of the most successful ways to use partners is at the computer. Sometimes there are not enough computers for each child to have one. In addition, there is too little time during the day to teach every student each activity or procedure on the computer. As soon as one child learns an activity, he or she can teach it to others. Working with a partner is not recommended when a student is using the word processor to write a story.

Using reading partners often works well. Any number of combinations is possible. Reading partners can be good friends on the same or a similar reading level. These partners work by reading to each other without the direct supervision of the teacher. One may read an entire story to the other, or they may choose to read every other page. One may ask the other to help with difficult words. Partners may listen to the tape of a story while reading along in copies of the book. Sometimes partners may evolve into larger groups of three or more if multiple copies of the taped books are available. Spontaneous choral reading, led by a strong reader,  breaks out in the Dramatic Play Center where all the children are seated together. Sometimes they read aloud with the tape. Books by Dr. Seuss and those that are students' favorites seem to stimulate this phenomenon. This is learning at its best. This type of partner grouping occurs in centers, open time (quiet, free-choice activities), and sometimes during silent reading and guided reading.

Partners can also be used in a mixed-age situation. Younger students can be assigned one or more mentors from the older group of students. During reading response, centers, and math lab, a student can be seated near the mentor to receive occasional help. They do not have to be working on the same project, but the mentor must be open to questions while working and stop to give assistance as needed. This is similar to tutoring, but the mentor can continue with his/her own work. The teacher must train the mentors to help the younger students by asking questions and guiding them toward conclusions rather than doing all the work for them. Some direct assistance is acceptable if accompanied by an explanation.

Beginning the Day

A Specific Routine

There should be a routine to begin each morning. Use the suggested schedule shown below or create your own. Display the schedule on a piece of poster board to let children know exactly what to do when they come in the door. You may wish to include pictures or symbols along with the written directions.

1. Put away your coat and backpack.
2. Turn in your homework folder to the homework file and/or home reader to the book-bag box.
3. Remove the clothespin from the attendance poster and place it on the graph poster, indicating whether you have brought a lunch or you are getting a cafeteria lunch. Place your money in a small envelope and give it to the teacher.
4. Choose a book from the classroom library for silent reading. (If the class includes kindergarten children, have them select books and put them in the kindergarten box to read later.)
5. Write the title of the book in your Reading Response Log. (Kindergarten students do not do this until the end of the year.)
6. Sign up for the morning centers or check the center assignment board. (Children do not choose centers for the first six weeks of school. They are assigned by the teacher.)

After the Morning Routine

- If there is time left after completing the morning routine, children may choose from several quiet activities. This is called *open time*, and the activities are free choice. Here are several ideas:
- Library Browse — The Library Center is open in the mornings.
- Brain Buster Activities — These are activities like estimating the number of beans in a jar, solving problems, analogies, challenging worksheets, graphs, etc. Students choosing to complete these activities receive rewards or recognition on a chart.
- Table Activities — These are small games and activities from the Reading/Skills Center that may be taken to a table for completion. These activities are available all day except when students are preparing to leave the room.
- Drawing Tablet — Each student keeps a drawing tablet in his/her cubby or desk. These can be teacher-made, using construction paper covers and newsprint pages, or commercially purchased.

The Teacher's Role

During this time the teacher reinforces the morning routines, takes up lunch money, assists in the selection of books for silent reading, supervises center selection during the sign-up process, and double checks the attendance and lunch count. After open time, the whole class begins language arts. See pages 30–50 for additional information about language arts.

Books, Books, Books

Using Literature with Theme-Based Teaching

One of the problems connected with theme-based instruction is not having enough books. You will probably need to make more trips to the library than you usually do. It is helpful to keep comprehensive book lists by theme. Keep careful records of the books you use during each month or grading period. Encourage your librarian to buy multiple copies of your favorite titles. If you have funds allocated to your classroom, use part of that money to buy multiple copies of hardback books with cassette tapes. Some titles are so popular that they are almost impossible to check out on a long-term basis. To accommodate a multi-age group of 20 to 24 children you will need at least 60 books. The school library may not be able to provide the books you need when you need them. Most teachers find it necessary to purchase additional books for their classrooms.

Inexpensive Ways to Acquire Books

There are many ways that you can acquire books for your classroom without spending large sums of money.

1. Investigate the possibility of applying for a special grant to buy books for your classroom. Create a special unit or project requiring multiple copies of your favorite titles.

2. Contact service organizations like the Lions Club or other community clubs to inquire about donations for books.

3. Ask for books that are being discarded from the school and public libraries.

4. Seek permission from your principal to hold a classroom fund raising activity for books.

5. Be first in line and take a large box when your school discards books from the bookroom.

6. Request books from friends and relatives whose children have outgrown them.

7. Send out letters to parents of former and/or present students, requesting donations of books (and games) their children have outgrown or no longer use.

8. Order multiple copies of paperbacks (with tapes when available), using the bonus points you accumulate by ordering from children's book clubs. Sometimes the book clubs offer hardback versions of the books, too. Although these are more expensive, they tend to be more durable.

9. Buy used books from a discount book store.

10. You might be able to make an agreement with a local retail book store to give you free samples of children's books if you have students use the books to write reviews, draw advertisements, or write story summaries that can be displayed in the store.

The Importance of Book Displays

It is not enough to have large numbers of books. They must be displayed in an attractive manner to stimulate interest. Listed below are some display ideas.

1. Plastic or cardboard magazine storage cases

2. One or two plastic cubes from discount stores

3. Small display cases (at least one per center) where the book covers can be seen

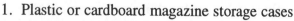

Special Books

Your Mission

You may need to stop once in a while and gaze into a crystal ball. Can you see your students' futures? Do you hear parents bragging about how much their children love books? If you love books and share those feelings with children, it is contagious. Here are a few tips to help your students become enamored with reading. There are books about which you feel strongly about. Make sure your feelings about special books are communicated to children. It takes just a few seconds to say things like:

- *I love this book. It won a prize for the art.*

- *When I saw this book I just had to buy it. I bought it especially to read to you because I knew you would like it.*

- *This was one of my favorite books when I was a little girl. My mother used to read it to me when I was six years old. I made her read it over and over, and then I would try to read it by myself.*

- *You will like this book because you will soon be able to read it all by yourself.*

Attitudes are usually more important than the skills. Students look to adults to form their opinions and preferences. Children who love books don't usually grow up to be poor readers. A few comments to students about the joy of literature may be far more important than hours of drill. Children are masters of imitation. Most teachers would be surprised to see some of their young students years later. Sometimes young students who appear apathetic are silently soaking up attitudes and building life-long habits. Children who seem to be completely without ability do learn to read. Some of them become avid readers.

Knowing How to Read Is Not Enough

It may be helpful to read street signs, maps, and job applications, but there should be more. In order to become truly educated, students must want to read. Phonics, grammar, and content are not the sum of reading. Teachers can accomplish much good with a few simple questions:

- *What books would you like to read?*

- *What would you like to learn about?*

- *What did you like or dislike about this book? How does it make you feel?*

Teachers must help students give voice to their feelings.

Special Books (cont.)

Literature-Based Instruction

Teachers who begin multi-age instruction soon turn their classrooms into small libraries. Literature-based instruction requires that students have access to a huge selection of books. The success of a theme will depend on the excitement generated by the books chosen for the unit. Shown below are two examples with literary suggestions for two thematic units.

Unit on Africa

- Introduce Nila K. Leigh's *Learning to Swim in Swaziland: A Child's-Eye View of a Southern African Country* (Scholastic, 1993) by saying, "I can't wait to show you this book. It will make you feel like you have been to Africa." This book is absolutely too good to miss. Begin with a map theme and follow up with an African theme. The book was written by an eight-year-old, providing endless opportunities for writing, illustrating, making scrapbooks, and taking pictures.

- Gather additional books about Africa. Be sure to include titles that are suitable for all reading levels in your class.

    For emergent readers:

    Feelings, Muriel L. *Jambo Means Hello: Swahili Alphabet Book.* Dial, 1974.

    Feelings, Muriel L. *Moja Means One.* Dial, 1971.

    For early fluent readers:

    Aardema, Verna. *Bringing the Rain to Kapiti Plain: A Nandi Tale.* Dial, 1981.

    For fluent readers:

    Musgrove, Margaret. *Ashanti to Zulu: African Traditions.* Dial, 1976. This book is available as a Big Book from Scholastic. It is a Caldecott winner with illustrations by the famous artists Leo and Diane Dillon.

Unit on Art/Beauty

- Children will not learn to see or appreciate art/beauty unless they are taught. Try to include a unit on art/beauty at least once a year. Students who are exposed to literature and art experiences will grow up to have clearer perceptions of the world around them. There are many experiences and resources from which to choose.

- Consider using these very special books:

    Bjork, Christina. *Linnea in Monet's Garden.* R&S Books, 1985.

    Ahensun, Aheng and Alice Low. *A Young Painter.* Scholastic, 1991.

    Both books are challenging, but you can share them with the class by reading them aloud.

- For an art unit that the children will always remember, bring in some books that show different types of art. Each year change the theme slightly with variations such as art in nature, the artist in you, or art in literature. Books that have won the Caldecott award for outstanding art would be good choices.

Developing Imagination

Using Literature to Develop Imagination

Use literature for the specific purpose of showing children how people use their imaginations. Begin by reading *Where the Wild Things Are* by Maurice Sendak (Harper, 1963). In the Listening/Author Center begin to study Maurice Sendak, the author. Provide several other books by Sendak. A good book for chapter book readers is *Higglety Pigglety Pop!* (Harper, 1967). The book stars Sendak's real dog named Jenny. This is an excellent example of how people use real things in their lives to create art and literature. Kindergartners can read *Hector Protector and As I Went Over the Water: Two Nursery Rhymes with Pictures* (Harper, 1965). Sendak is one of the inventors of predictable books. *Chicken Soup with Rice* (Harper, 1962) is an excellent example of a predictable book. This story is available as a Big Book, making it perfect for first graders. To extend a literary theme, take it to a higher level by encouraging children to use their imaginations the way Sendak does. Open-ended creative activities build self-esteem and encourage appropriate risk taking because there are no wrong or right answers. Here are some suggested activities.

- **Activity 1:** Draw/write about an imaginary land as Maurice Sendak did in *Where the Wild Things Are*. What does it look like? Is it a town, a rain forest, or under the sea? What colors do you see there? What sounds do you hear?

- **Activity 2:** Create some creatures to live in your imaginary place. What do they look like? How do they feel? What do they like to do? Draw these creatures and make them into paper dolls by gluing them onto cardboard. Write or tell about how they look, feel, and act. Be sure to give plenty of descriptive details.

- **Activity 3:** Take the paper dolls you made in Activity 2 to a center and play with them. Draw background scenery for them by creating a mural or by gluing pictures to a sheet of butcher paper. Give names to the creatures and make up stories about them. By yourself or with one or two other students, write a story about the creatures. Then present the story to the class, record it on a tape, or make a chart that shows the characters, setting, and events.

- **Activity 4:** What would the creatures eat in an imaginary land? Work with a group of students to draw the creatures' food and glue it onto paper plates. Pretend the Home/Dramatic Play Center is a restaurant and serve the plates of food to your guests. The customers could ask the waiter how the food tastes or smells. Prepare menus with pictures and descriptions. Give cooking lessons. You may wish to create special money for your creatures to use.

- **Activity 5:** Work with a group to prepare an art exhibit and/or a musical composition from an imaginary place. What would the art look like or the music sound like? What kind of materials would be used to create the art? Would there be lyrics to the music?

Developing Thinking Skills

Real life consists of one problem after another. Children can practice solving problems in real and make-believe situations through the use of literature. Good answers can be logical, unusual, or even funny. The key is to appreciate the creativity in all answers rather than trying to find the one correct answer. If done orally as a class or in a small group, each answer can be briefly discussed. If used as a writing assignment for older students, schedule a feedback conference with individual students to show appreciation for each child's ideas.

- *Sylvester and the Magic Pebble* by William Steig (Simon, 1980) is perfect to teach prediction. Read the book to the whole class but stop when the lion meets Sylvester on the hill. Ask the following: Will Sylvester be eaten by the lion? What can he do? Do not remind the children that Sylvester is holding a magic pebble because some of their solutions could be practical, rather than magical. Accept and briefly discuss all suggestions. Finish reading the book. As a follow-up activity, you may wish to have younger students draw pictures of their ideas while older students write and draw theirs.

- *The Amazing Bone*, also by William Steig (Farrar, 1976), offers another prediction opportunity when the fox locks Pearl in a room and prepares to eat her. Ask the following: Will Pearl be eaten by the fox? Can anyone help? What can Pearl do? Related books that show a means of escape from certain doom are *Bony-legs* by Johanna Cole (Four Winds Press, 1983) and *Baba Yaga: A Russian Folk tale* by Eric A. Kimmel (Holiday, 1991). Perhaps all three could be used in a theme about magic or fantasy. As a follow-up activity, you may wish to urge older students to create and write their own stories, such as *Trapped in Dragon Valley* or *I Traveled Back in Time to Find a Dinosaur Egg*. The endings could be left open on some of these stories so that the author could ask the class to suggest some solutions/conclusions.

- *Harold and the Purple Crayon* by Crockett Johnson (HarperCollins, 1955) is a perfect example of creative thinking. Stop the story when Harold falls off the other side of the mountain while holding his purple crayon. Kindergartners can answer orally to solve the problem. Then later they can draw pictures to show details from the book. Older children can draw their solutions. Second graders can write their answers, perhaps listing several solutions. This makes a good reading response.

- *Curious George* by H. A. Rey (Houghton Mifflin, 1969) begins with the man in the yellow hat trying to catch George, who is a little monkey in a tree. Read the whole book first and then have the children imagine that the man does not have a yellow hat. Let them create ways to catch George. To begin, do not allow them to answer orally. Instead, have them draw pictures. Non-readers can stop with the pictures; readers can write a few sentences explaining their pictures. Then encourage all students to share their pictures and ideas with the class. This fits well in a zoo or animal theme. In other books, George visits farms, circuses, space, and the alphabet.

Books Too Good to Miss

Aardema, Vera. *Why Mosquitoes Buzz in People's Ears.* Dial Books for Young Readers, 1978.

Ahlberg, Janet and Allan. *Each Peach Pear Plum.* Scholastic, 1978.

Allard, Harry and James Marshall. *Miss Nelson Has a Field Day.* Houghton Mifflin, 1985.

Allard, Harry and James Marshall. *Miss Nelson Is Back.* Houghton Mifflin, 1982.

Allard, Harry and James Marshall. *Miss Nelson Is Missing.* Scholastic, 1977.

Barrett, Judi. *Animals Should Definitely Not Wear Clothing.* Aladdin, 1980.

Bemelmans, Ludwig. *Madeline.* Viking, 1967.

Brown, Margarite Wise. *The Runaway Bunny.* Harper, 1972.

Brunhoff, Jean de. *The Story of Babar, the Little Elephant.* Knopf, 1933.

Brunhoff, Jean de. *The Travels of Babar.* Knopf, 1934.

Campbell, Rod. *Dear Zoo.* Penguin (Puffin), 1982.

Carle, Eric. *Have You Seen My Cat?* Eric Carle Corp., 1987.

Cherry, Lynne. *The Great Kapok Tree.* HBJ, 1990.

Cleary, Beverly. *Ramona and Her Father; Ramona and Her Mother; Ramona Forever; Ramona Quimby, Age 8; Ramona the Brave; Ramona the Pest.* Morrow, 1968–1984.

Cole, Joanna. *Bony-legs.* Four Winds Press, 1983.

Dahl, Roald. *James and the Giant Peach: A Children's Story.* Knopf, 1961.

Degen, Bruce. *Jamberry.* Harper, 1983.

Ehlert, Lois. *Eating the Alphabet: Fruits and Vegetables from A to Z.* HBJ, 1989.

Ehlert, Lois. *Growing Vegetable Soup.* HBJ, 1987.

Estes, Eleanor. *The Hundred Dresses.* HBJ, 1944.

Ets, Marie Hall and Aurora Labastida. *Nine Days to Christmas.* Viking, 1959.

Flack, Marjorie. *The Story About Ping.* Viking, 1933.

Gag, Wanda. *Millions of Cats.* Putnam, 1977.

Galdone, Paul. *The Little Red Hen.* Houghton Mifflin, 1985.

Gardiner, John R. *Stone Fox.* Harper & Row, 1983.

Gilman, Phoebe. *Grandma and the Pirates.* Scholastic, 1990.

Grahame, Kenneth. *The Wind in the Willows.* Macmillan, 1989.

Hall, Donald. *The Ox-Cart Man.* Penguin, 1983.

Henkes, Kevin. *Owen.* Greenwillow, 1993.

Kalan, Robert. *Jump, Frog, Jump!* Greenwillow, 1981.

Books Too Good to Miss (cont.)

Leaf, Munro. *The Story of Ferdinand.* Viking, 1936.

Lewis, C.S. *The Lion, the Witch, and the Wardrobe.* Harper, 1950.

Lobel, Arnold and Anita. *On Market Street.* Greenwillow, 1981.

Lyon, George. *Come a Tide.* Orchard Books, 1990.

MacDonald, Golden. *The Little Island.* Dell Yearling, 1993.

Martin, Bill. *Brown Bear, Brown Bear, What Do You See?* Holt, Rinehart & Winston, 1992.

Martin, Bill. *Chicka Chicka Boom Boom.* Simon & Schuster, 1989.

McCloskey, Robert. *Blueberries for Sal.* Viking, 1976.

McCloskey, Robert. *Make Way for Ducklings.* Viking, 1941.

McCloskey, Robert. *One Morning in Maine.* Viking, 1980.

Melmed, Laura Krauss. *The Rainbabies.* Lothrop, Lee, & Shepard, 1992.

Minarik, Else Holmelund. *Little Bear.* Harper & Row, 1957.

Ness, Evaline. *Sam, Bangs, and Moonshine.* Holt, Rinehart & Winston, 1966.

Scieszka, Jon. *The True Story of the Three Little Pigs.* Viking, 1992.

Seuss, Dr. *The Cat in the Hat.* Random, 1957.

Seuss, Dr. *Green Eggs and Ham.* Random, 1960.

Seuss, Dr. *How the Grinch Stole Christmas.* Random, 1957.

Seuss, Dr. *Horton Hears a Who.* Random, 1954.

Silverstein, Shel. *The Giving Tree.* Harper, 1964.

Silverstein, Shel. *A Light in the Attic.* Harper, 1981.

Silverstein, Shel. *Where the Sidewalk Ends.* Harper, 1974.

Slepian, Jan and Ann Seidler. *The Cat Who Wore a Pot on Her Head;* (Original Title: *Bendemolena*). Scholastic, 1967.

Thurber, James. *Many Moons.* HBJ, 1943.

Van Allsburg, Chris. *The Garden of Abdul Gasazi.* Houghton Mifflin, 1979.

Van Allsburg, Chris. *Jumanji.* Houghton Mifflin, 1981.

Van Allsburg, Chris. *The Polar Express.* Houghton Mifflin, 1985.

White, E.B. *Charlotte's Web.* Harper & Row, 1952.

Wilder, Laura Ingalls. *Little House on the Prairie.* Harper & Row, 1953.

Williams, Margery. *The Velveteen Rabbit.* Avon, 1975.

Some of these books may be out of print. However, they can still be found in many public and school libraries.

Poetry is often easier for children to read because of the meter and rhyme. In addition, some children who are not interested in reading will surprise you and respond enthusiastically to poetry. Look in the poetry section of your school or public library for poems by Shel Silverstein, Lewis Carroll, Jack Prelutsky, Ogden Nash, and Laura Richards. You may also wish to ask the librarian for an anthology.

Whole Language

What Is Whole Language?

1. In whole language, skills and activities are arranged around a literary experience. For example, children can learn about the letter Ss while studying Jane Taylor's *Twinkle, Twinkle, Little Star* (Scholastic, 1992). The teacher emphasizes that learning the *s* sound will help them read words like *star* and *sun*. Whole-language instruction means that reading, writing, spelling, and speaking are not taught in separate subjects but are related to a particular story or poem. Science, art, and math units are coordinated with the literature selection. Children who are reading *Twinkle, Twinkle, Little Star* should also learn about space through science, math, and art.

2. Meaning is emphasized in whole language but not by asking questions about the story or poem. The class is immersed in meaning by repeated experiences that include discussions, art projects, sequencing activities, and the cloze procedure by which context clues are used to determine word meanings. It is desirable for students to memorize their favorite selections. They should experience literature through dramatization and play. Young children often learn best by retelling a poem or story with flannel board figures. As a result, a flannel board and figures should be readily available in one of the centers. A copy of the text should also be provided. Children may choose to act out the poem or story in the Block Center or the Home/Dramatic Play Center. You will need a second set of flannel board figures for whole-class presentations.

3. In whole language, students use library books or Big Books instead of traditional textbooks. However, you may wish to use your textbooks if they contain high-quality literature selections. Vocabulary is not introduced and defined before reading the story. The story is read for enjoyment before analysis.

4. Creative writing is important. Children use ideas or patterns from the story to create new stories. Younger children will need additional guidance, suggestions, and feedback to develop their creative writing skills.

5. Students use approximated or invented spelling during creative writing. They should be encouraged to sound out words and spell them as well as possible. Emphasizing correct spelling may intimidate very young writers. Older students can revise and edit their first drafts to eliminate mechanical errors such as spelling mistakes.

6. Children are immersed in print in a whole-language classroom. Walls and bulletin boards are covered with labeled pictures and creative writing. Copies of student books, library books, and Big Books are available in the reading area. Children learn in centers with activities related to stories or nursery rhymes. Learning is informal and often designed by students. Lecture time is reduced, and student participation in activities is increased. Children often appear to be playing, but they are really learning by doing. Consequently, test results are often a pleasant surprise.

Metacognition

What Is Metacognition?

Metacognition is quite simply thinking about thinking. In schools, metacognition seems to be specifically thinking about learning and how to learn most effectively. When working with young children, metacognition consists of the following aspects.

1. Make children aware of the processes they go through to successfully learn something. Metacognition emphasizes process as well as the finished product. It is assumed that if children are aware of how they learn, they will be more likely to repeat successful behaviors.

2. Encourage students to talk and write about how they learn things and how they do things. The key word here is *how*. If teachers consistently ask how things are done, it becomes a short cut to higher levels of thinking and understanding. Questions that ask *how* and *why* automatically produce higher level thinking processes than questions that begin with *who, where,* and *when.*

3. Have children share their successful strategies for learning with each other through the use of cooperative learning groups and presentations. You will notice that presentations offer students the opportunity to organize their thinking. Students practice describing their activities in sequence. Presentations also emphasize how to look at things from a conceptual point of view rather than as a disconnected group of facts. In the multi-age classroom, observation of one student by another shows younger children how the older ones go about the process of learning.

4. Students can plan how to learn. Metacognition can be improved by simply asking a few questions and recording the responses. Some questions to try include: What would you like to learn about? Where can we find information about this topic? How can we find out about this topic?

Application of Metacognition

The challenge of metacognition is how to apply it so that it is meaningful and interesting to young children. Here are some simple steps to begin.

1. Teacher observation and anecdotal records will help encourage children to use successful learning behaviors. As you go about the business of recording student achievement, you are also modeling observational techniques for the children to imitate. You may wish to have students learn how to record behaviors by observing you as you teach. Then the students can make observations of their own.

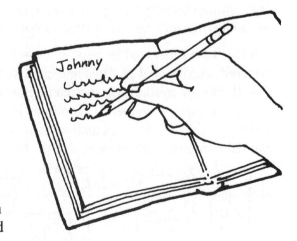

2. Older students who are mentors and tutors can plan lessons for the younger children. They can prepare teaching aids that show the steps needed to learn a skill.

How to Get Started

You Can Do It!

You may be surprised at the success you will achieve by working with students in a multi-age setting. Many of the skills and materials that you already have will continue to be useful.

Retain practices that are comfortable for you. If you are currently using three reading groups, do not try to abandon them immediately. Some teachers who have been teaching multi-age classrooms for years are still using three reading groups. It may be necessary to change your schedule a bit. It is best to have reading instruction in the morning, allowing for the usual interruptions of scheduled classes: physical education, music, art, library, etc. Start every morning with the reading group that needs the most help. When you finish with that group, call another. If time allows, you may wish to call additional groups. However, some mornings you might have time to work only with two groups.

You can also continue to use textbooks if you are currently using them. Just coordinate the story selections with a theme or topic. Add an additional subject like art. For example, if your class is reading *Rosie's Walk* by Pat Hutchins (Aladdin, 1968), plan an art project related to the story.

The Next Step-Scheduling Reading Groups

Adjust the number of reading groups to suit you. Most multi-age teachers have **three** to **five** reading groups. You may wish to continue with three reading groups so that you will feel comfortable about how many times you meet with each group. The schedule below is for reading groups in a classroom that has first and second grade students. *Emergent readers* are students in the readiness stage and those beginning to read a few words and sentences. *Early fluent readers* are the students who used to be called the middle group. They will include some first graders and some second graders. *Fluent readers* will be mostly second graders. These children are capable of reading and understanding most easy readers and simple library books with only occasional assistance. Some can read chapter books.

Monday: *Emergent Readers, Early Fluent Readers*

Tuesday: *Emergent Readers, Fluent Readers*

Wednesday: *Emergent Readers, Early Fluent Readers*

Thursday: *Emergent Readers, Fluent Readers*

Friday: *Emergent Readers, Early Fluent Readers*

Use the remainder of the morning to walk around the classroom, instructing individuals on procedures. Teach center management and listen to individuals read. Some students will read from textbooks or trade books; others will read their own creations or reading responses. This procedure is called *student conferencing*. Shortly before the end of the language arts block, children clean up and come together to present their projects and discuss their activities.

Language Arts Time

The Literary Arts

Language arts instruction contains all the components of literacy: reading, speaking, writing, and spelling. The block of time designated for language arts is in the morning, directly after the procedures described on page 23, Beginning the Day. Do not worry if physical education, recess, music, art, or other scheduled classes interrupt the language arts block. Simply leave everything as it is and go to the other class. When you return, continue where you left off. Language arts may spill over into the afternoon, but this should not present a problem. **Approximately two hours should be scheduled for the language arts block each day.** The time frame may be broken down as follows:

---

1. Shared reading and lessons for the whole class

2. Reading time or sustained silent reading

3. Work period in centers and in small groups

4. Student presentations and sharing

The Language Arts Block

The language arts block replaces the time spent with reading groups in traditional classrooms. It differs in several ways:

1. Instead of children going to their desks while other groups read, they go to the centers.

2. The time referred to as *sustained silent reading* in other publications has been integrated into the reading lesson. Perhaps a better title for this activity would be *reading time*.

3. Workbooks are not used. Children respond to literature in a variety of ways by writing, drawing, and creating projects. All children except kindergartners are required to respond to literature on a daily basis. This is done individually, but additional projects may be completed by groups in the centers.

4. Reading groups or flexible groups can be assembled during this time. **All groups may not meet with the teacher every day.** Teachers may spend time listening to individuals read or evaluating writing. Small exchanges and tutoring sessions are called *student conferences*. These are often documented for the evaluation portfolio.

5. After center time, students discuss their work and present projects to the class. This provides an opportunity for the oral language component. It is also an excellent time for teachers to evaluate students.

Language Arts Time (cont.)

A Typical Morning

It is assumed throughout this book that language arts is scheduled during the morning as it is in most schools. However, there are instances where math and science might be taught in the mornings. Each teacher should arrange the schedule as convenient or as school policy dictates.

The focus of the first six weeks is spent on training and orientation. The following information describes a typical morning that would occur any time after the first six weeks.

Whole-Class Lesson

- The teacher reads aloud, perhaps a poem and then a predictable book. Sometimes she/he simply reads a book that students will read later. The time frame for this lesson varies with the length of the book. If the book is exceptionally long, the teacher can finish it the next day or in read-aloud time after lunch.

- Reading aloud is followed by a quick lesson. It is important that you do not spend a great deal of time on the lesson. Explain the behavior or skill to be taught and then quickly demonstrate it. As the school year progresses, this portion of the lesson should not last over ten minutes. Students who do not comprehend can be tutored in small groups or during individual conferences.

- Damage control discussions can cover any area that seems to be affecting more than one member of the class. It is important to deal with problems before children begin their small-group and center activities for the day. Topics might include: skills, classroom procedures, or discipline. The time limit for this type of discussion should be about five minutes.

Reading Time or Sustained Silent Reading

- Students locate the book they have chosen to read and begin silent reading. The emergent readers usually have reading time at the teacher's table. They have already placed their chosen books on the table during the morning preparation time. It is often necessary for the teacher to help students in this group choose books that they are capable of reading.

- The teacher begins small-group instruction with the group at his/her table. Other children are still reading to themselves. They begin center activities after finishing their books or when the teacher says that it is the end of the time allowed. When the teacher finishes with the emergent readers, they go to centers. The teacher calls another group.

- After the second group, the teacher moves about the classroom conferencing, observing, and making notes. Near the end of the morning, students clean up and make presentations. The teacher makes notes again during presentations. The language arts block lasts about two hours.

Reading Response

Daily Response

Every child in the classroom responds to the silent reading selection on paper every day. This does not include kindergarten children who respond mostly by participating in center activities (pages 61-113) and only occasionally on paper. The best way to organize reading responses is have each child use a three- or five- subject, spiral-bound notebook.

Easing into Responses

To begin daily responses, have students try a few easy ones such as those described below and on page 37.

1. **The title of my book is _____ .**

   Talk about the parts of a book: cover or front, spine, back. Show the covers of several books to locate the titles and to distinguish them from the names of the authors. Point out the title page inside the book. Demonstrate how to correctly copy the title of the book in the reading response notebook. Offer optional extension activities. Many students will want to write the name of the author, as well. They also like to draw the cover of the book. Instead of meeting with reading groups the first six weeks, monitor the centers and carefully evaluate reading responses.

   Conference with each child about the response by having her/him explain and read it to you. You may wish to have emergent readers point to each word to indicate that they can track and identify words. Advanced students should be expected to extend their responses if they have done reading response in previous years. During the first six weeks, it is especially important to conference about reading response and check the notebooks every day. Some evaluations can be written or done very quickly.

2. **My favorite picture is _____ .**

   Emphasize that the title must be written on every reading response so that people will know which book has the picture. Younger students can trace or draw the picture. Early fluent readers may be able to write a short description of the picture, such as, "My favorite picture was the forest in Max's room." These students can also tell why they liked the picture. If possible, kindergartersn and emergent readers can dictate their reasons for you to record. Accept any explanation.

3. **A character I like is _____. Why? _____ .**

   Younger children may simply draw the character. An alternate method is to list the characters in response to a question. Example: Who is in the book? The characters in the book were _____ . Such questions may be too difficult for some emergent readers to answer independently. In that case, reading response may be done as a guided lesson in small groups.

4. **My favorite part of the book is _____. Why? _____ .**

   A more appropriate form for younger children might be:
   The part I liked best was _____ .

Reading Response (cont.)

5. **This book is about _____ . Why?**

   Children should learn that this question may be asked in various forms. Example: The main idea of the book is _____ .

6. **A place in the book I would like to go is _____ . Why?**

   An alternate question is: The setting of the book is _____ .

7. **Another title for the book could be _____ . Why?**

8. **The book is a (real, make-believe) story. Why?**

   A more advanced form would be to have students distinguish between fiction and non fiction elements of the story.

9. **This is what happens at the end of the book. Why?**

10. **The story problem is _____. Why? _____ .**

11. **This book made me feel _____. Why? _____ .**

12. **This book made me think of _____. Why? _____ .**

Evaluations

After the first six weeks, evaluations of the reading response logs should be done as follows:

1. You should evaluate the reading response log every day for children who are having difficulty. Children who are emergent readers also need to have their reading response logs evaluated on a daily basis. This is not difficult since many of the guided lessons for this group involve reading response. Evaluations can be done during reading group at the teacher's table.

2. The notebooks of students who are doing satisfactory work can be checked every other day. This group includes most of the first grade children and early fluent readers.

3. Fluent readers' notebooks can be checked once a week. When fluent readers have mastered all the responses and can respond correctly to most curriculum skills, they substitute other forms of writing for reading response. Other forms might include journal writing, story writing, poetry, plays, descriptions, or critical evaluations of literature, film, or video.

Reading Response (cont.)

Advanced Reading Response

As long as testing is done in schools, curriculum will be test driven. To an extent, this is as it should be because children should be tested on what they are taught. You will need to write questions that reflect testing specifics. Reading responses can be tailored to match the curriculum. Simply study your district's curriculum guidelines and write a question for each topic.

Some areas covered might include:

- Prediction
- Classification
- Comparison
- Vocabulary Meaning
- Main Idea
- Details
- Fact and Opinion
- Cause-and-Effect Relationships
- Summarization
- Sequencing Events
- Story or Character Analysis
- Parts of Speech

As children master these skills, more difficult responses can be attempted. Some examples are shown below.

1. What does this book mean?

2. What is the author trying to say?

3. I like (or dislike) this book because _____ .

4. I agree (or disagree) with the author about _____ . Why?

5. If you could change the ending of the book, what would happen?

6. If you could change the setting of the book, what would it be?

7. If you could continue the story, what do you think would happen next?

8. Make up a story using the same (pattern, setting, characters).

9. Create art that shows how this book makes you feel.

10. Rewrite the story, using your own words.

Reading Response (cont.)

Presenting Reading Response

Write the response sentence(s) on a chalkboard or dry mark board. Write as large as possible because the youngest children need to see very large print. Students should copy a response sentence and finish it in their own words. Just writing the missing part of the sentence is not acceptable. After students have completed their responses, you should transfer them to sentence strips so that they can be used in a pocket chart.

Reading Response Forms

Several response forms (pages 41-43) and a Reading Response Log (page 44) are provided to meet individual needs. The first two response forms are for illustration responses, one with handwriting lines and one without. Use the one without lines unless a child has extremely poor handwriting or is very young. When working with very young children, you may wish to lightly write the child's dictation and let the child copy or trace it with a fine-tip marker. Children who insist that they cannot draw a picture about the book should be encouraged to trace one that exists in the book. Then slowly assure them that they can make up their own pictures to go with the story. Point out that their pictures do not have to look like the ones in the book. It is often helpful to present the same story with the art done by two different illustrators. In addition, children should have the opportunity to view posters of fine art that were created using many different styles. Looking at primitive art and modern art sometimes lessens their inhibitions. If the space at the bottom of the response form does not allow enough room, encourage students to continue on the back or begin a new page on a blank sheet of paper.

Storing Responses

If the class is using spiral notebooks, students may glue, tape, or staple the forms onto the pages in their notebooks. As they mature, they will learn to copy the reading response directly into the notebooks. They will also learn to adapt the size and page length to meet their individual needs. Some readers may wish to make several drawings and write a response that fills two or more pages. An alternative method for storing responses is to use three-ring binders. Provide copies of all the response forms in baskets. Prepare the forms for the binders by asking a volunteer or older student to use a three-hole punch.

Recording Responses

Each morning students can write their book choices for sustained silent reading in their Reading Response Logs (page 44). Several copes of this form can be glued in the front section of each large spiral notebook or placed in each ring binder. Children with large handwriting may use two lines. Kindergartners do not fill out the Reading Response Logs until they are beginning to read, which usually occurs in the middle of the year or later. A similar form (page 53) is available for home readers with a place for the parent to sign and make comments. These forms can be stapled to students' take-home folders.

Reading Response (cont.)

Managing Reading Response

Most children will do the reading response immediately after sustained silent reading. They may move to whatever part of the room necessary to complete the response. Students doing an illustration response may wish to move to the Art/Publishing Center. Since students sign up for centers when they arrive in the morning, many will choose to do their sustained silent reading and response in the chosen center. Students do not have assigned seats, so any part of the classroom is acceptable. Intervene only if there is overcrowding in a particular area or discipline problems arise.

Teaching Reading Response

Each day present a quick 10-15 minute lesson to the whole class. Introduce reading response during the quick lesson. During the first few days of school, choose one simple response and present it to the class. The quick lesson consists of an explanation and then a demonstration of a reading response. Choose a very simple book such as *Little Red Riding Hood.* (There are several versions of this Grimm Brothers' fairy tale.) Record the response on a chart and save it for next year. The entire class will be assigned the same reading response for the day. Even though the students all have the same assignment, the answers will be different for most students because they will be responding to different books. Kindergartners will be exempt from reading response on some days and can respond with a drawing on others. If some of the

centers have manipulatives for *Little Red Riding Hood,* kindergartners can respond through play. Suggested manipulatives include: puppets, dolls, magnetic figures, or flannel board figures. As you observe in each center, ask questions and make suggestions to stretch students' imaginations. For example, point out an African doll and a stuffed lion and ask how the story would be different if Little Red Riding Hood lived in Africa. Students who have been in the multi-age classroom in previous years should review reading responses the first six weeks.

Evaluating and Remediating Reading Response

Check students' responses each day. You may decide that you need to repeat the same response the following day. It is not uncommon to have the same reading response for two or three days in a row. Simply choose a different book to demonstrate with each time. After the second or third day, those children not ready to respond independently in writing can do their reading response with you during reading group. Children needing individual help might be tutored by teaching assistants, student teachers, volunteers, special education teachers, or by you during center time. Sometimes these children will need to respond with a drawing until their skills and self-confidence develop.

Reading Response — Form 1

Name: _____ Date: _____

Title: _____

Author: _____

Draw a picture.

Reading Response:

_____

_____

_____

_____

_____

_____

_____

_____

Reading Response — Form 2

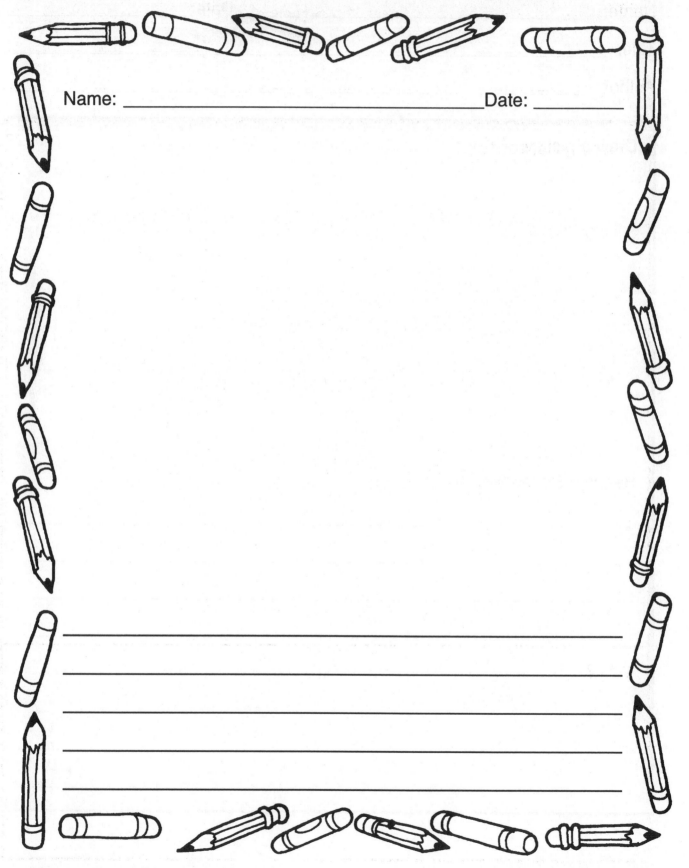

Name: _____ Date: _____

Reading Response — Form 3

Name:_____ Date: _____

Title: _____

Author: _____

Reading Response:

Why?

Reading Response Log

Name: _____

Date	Title	Author

Reading Choices

Begin with Silent Reading

Selecting a book to read is a skill that must be taught. As with all skills, some children will learn more quickly than others. The first step for you is to pretend to be a student selecting a book and model the process for the class in a quick lesson. This should be done sometime during the first day or two of school. Following the quick lesson, students should attempt to select their own books for the sustained silent reading session. The student selects a book each morning and uses it to do a written reading response. The silent reading selection is often used for reading group too.

Monitor Student Selections

During the first six weeks, try to evaluate each child's ability to select a book for silent reading. Ideally students should pick books that they can read independently. This does not mean that students have to be able to read every word, just that they must be able to read their chosen books well enough to gain meaning and then write their responses. Part of your time during the morning routine should be used to assist students with their choices. Later in the morning, have individuals read to you from their book selections during reading group or afterward in centers.

Sustained Silent Reading

At the beginning of the year, students may not have the stamina, ability, or interest to read silently for any length of time. The silent reading period may only last 10–15 minutes. As the year progresses, the session should slowly lengthen until students are reading for about 30 minutes. A problem may arise when students who do not read well finish quickly and are done long before the sustained silent reading time is over. These are students that need special attention during the book selection time. Those students who are only able to read 2-5 short books may need to have five very easy books packaged together in a zippered plastic bag. Students with short attention spans or limited reading ability can do their silent reading at the teacher table so as not to disturb other students. When silent reading is completed, this group can begin a guided lesson while the more fluent readers continue to read silently. Often it is necessary for emergent readers to read several books during the silent reading time because the stories are so short. **The guided reading selection for the emergent readers can be one of the stories they used for silent reading.**

Guided Reading Selection

Some teachers select the guided reading material for their students. At the first of the year, all teachers should make the selections. If the whole group is reading the same book, student choice can begin by allowing the group to vote on two choices that you have pre-selected. As the abilities of the group increase, so can the range of choices. The goal is to have individuals who can choose their own reading material for enjoyment or information.

Managing Guided Reading

Individual Styles

For many teachers, guided reading will be much like traditional reading groups. If you are accustomed to whole language, your guided groups will contain all the hallmarks of good whole-language teaching. Teachers should move slowly when attempting to make changes in successful teaching styles. There may be many occasions when you need to use the stories from the basal reader for guided group instruction. Note that basal readers are now called anthologies. If the story quality is good, it should not matter what book is used. One thing that will be different in the multi-age classroom is the record keeping. When all children read the same basals, it was easier to keep track of which stories or books had been read. This is no longer true, and extensive record keeping is necessary in most of today's classrooms. A multi-age classroom, or any classroom using whole language, moves students toward individualization with reading selections made by each child.

Reading Record Forms

You may wish to use the Reading Record form (page 48) to assess guided reading. This form is divided into six sections so that observations can be recorded once each week for six weeks. Although teachers make observations daily, no one has time to write them for every child every day, nor is anyone interested in reading them. Documentation is necessary, but it is easy for beginners to go overboard. Try to look at the big picture. The forms can also be used for individual reading conferences and tutoring sessions. These can be completed while students are at centers and sometimes during silent reading. **Try to do about four or five written observations during the language arts block each day.** Sometimes it is easier to write them on tiny stick-on notes and transfer them to the Reading Record later.

Reading Record

Student's Name: _____

Date	Title and Author	Observations

Language Arts Anecdotal Record

The Language Arts Anecdotal Record (page 51) is designed so that it will hold six 3" x 3" stick-on notes. Use of the Anecdotal Record is flexible. It might be used to comment on weekly journal writing or to indicate test results or skills mastered. Note that it is possible to modify the form to specifically indicate certain skills. Cover the headings that indicate the weeks in the grading period and substitute the names of skills. In each square, write reading or language skills such as contractions, blends, sequencing, retelling a story, or writing in complete sentences. To make the Anecdotal Record more specific, write a label such as *Writing Skills* or *Pre-reading Skills* above the space labeled *Grading Period*. Place each child's Anecdotal Record and Reading Record in his/her evaluation folder.

Reading Groups

The Perfect Classroom

In the perfect classroom there are no reading groups. There may be some flexible groups, but not everyone participates in a reading group. Reading groups exist for the purpose of student evaluation and practice. There are other ways to accomplish this. Students can practice their reading skills away from the teacher. An alternate method of student evaluation is the individual conference. This type of conference can be quick and informal, or it can be a comprehensive assessment with checklists and goal setting. For the informal conference, sit by the student's desk and ask the student to read a sentence, paragraph, or page from a book or from his/her own writing. Then ask a question or two to determine the student's understanding. Assessment is then recorded on a stick-on note or on page 50 especially designed for quick observations and anecdotes. See the sample form on page 49. Using the Observation Form ensures that all students are evaluated on a weekly basis. Three pages with names are fastened to a clipboard so you can quickly see which students need conferences. The sheets are cut apart and taped or glued in the student portfolios at the end of the week. Evaluation also includes testing, listening to partners read, and making notations during project presentations. You may also wish to review notebooks and papers as a means of evaluation.

Fluent Readers

This group usually consists of second grade children who are returning to a multi-age classroom for the second or third year. After some review of the skills at the first of the year, students often work independently on projects. The fluent readers choose their own reading materials, and some fluent readers complete reading responses. Others who are capable of more responsibility, may be writing stories or plays or creating new games. The fluent reader designation is certainly not limited to second graders. Fluent readers may be first graders and occasionally kindergartners. All fluent readers complete reading responses daily until they have shown mastery of the responses and skills. At this time, self-starters are given more independence.

Book Clubs

All fluent readers are encouraged to join reading discussion groups that are very similar to adult reading clubs. The group chooses a book or a series of books and meets once a week or more often if they choose. The groups meet during center time on set days. At first, you will lead the group in a manner similar to an informal guided lesson. Later, if students are really interested in the reading material, the groups will be led by students. Then you become a participant or simply an observer. This provides you with an excellent opportunity to record observations for evaluation purposes.

Reading Record

Student's Name: _____

Date	Title and Author	Observations

48   © Teacher Created Materials, Inc.

Observation Form — Sample

Reproduce the blank Observation Form (page 50). Use this page as a guide to filling out the blank forms.

Joe Doe	Jane No	Abe Lincoln
He has discovered punctuation. He is putting periods after every word. Sept. 96	She wrote a long story today. It was about her cat. I helped her choose the title, "My Cat." Sept. 96	He read *Brown Bear*, played with the felt cutouts, and then asked for more books. Sept. 96
Marco Polo	John Adams	Ben Frank
After looking at an atlas, he drew a map. He wrote "MAP" at the top of the drawing. Sept. 96	John read a story from *Little Bear* and drew pictures. Sept. 96	He copied a model of the solar system into his notebook. Sept. 96
Susan Anthony	Bo Peep	Bob Blue
She drew a flag and wrote "U.S.A." on the paper. Sept. 96	She recited and sang several nursery rhymes, such as *Humpty Dumpty* and *Little Boy Blue.* Sept. 96	His group began reading *Stone Fox* today. Sept. 96

Observation Form

1. Reproduce this page. Make as many copies as you need.

2. Type or write one student's name in each square.

3. Place the forms on a clipboard so that you can make notes of things you observe while moving around the classroom.

4. Date, cut apart, and tape the section of the form completed for each student in his or her file.

Anecdotal Record

Student's Name: _____   Grading Period: _____

First Week	Second Week	Third Week
Fourth Week	Fifth Week	Sixth Week

Home Reading Log — Sample

Dear Parents,

Please complete and sign the following form.

Thank you,

_____

Teacher's Signature

Student's Name: Jerome Anderson

Title: *Dear Zoo*   **Date: 10-3**

Comments: He was so excited. He read the book to us as soon as he got home. He read it several times. Please send a new book.

Parent Signature: *Mrs. Jones*

Title: *Jump, Frog, Jump!*   **Date: 10-23**

Comments: He tried to read the book two times the first night, but he had trouble with a few pages. He did very well the second night.

Parent Signature: *Mrs. Jones*

Title: *Have You Seen My Cat?*   **Date: 11-4**

Comments: He read this book easily.

Parent Signature: *Mrs. Jones*

Title: *The Little Red Hen*   **Date: 11-8**

Comments: We worked on this book for four nights. He can read it now.

Parent Signature: *Mrs. Jones*

Title: *Jamberry*   **Date: 11-20**

Comments: This is a short book, and he wanted to read it. I think some words are too hard so we read it together.

Parent Signature: *Mrs. Jones*

Title: *Green Eggs and Ham*   **Date: 12-1**

Comments: We read this book for two nights. He reads it pretty well, but he is still missing a few words.

Parent Signature: *Mrs. Jones*

Home Reading Log

Dear Parents,

Please complete and sign the following form.

Thank you,

_____

Teacher's Signature

Student's Name: _____

Title: **Date:**

Comments:

Parent Signature:

Title: **Date:**

Comments:

Parent Signature:

Title: **Date:**

Comments:

Parent Signature:

Title: **Date:**

Comments:

Parent Signature:

Title: **Date:**

Comments:

Parent Signature:

Title: **Date:**

Comments:

Parent Signature:

Changing Math Instruction

Our Mathematical Roots

One of the main thrusts for change began in England over thirty years ago with the origin of the Nuffield Mathematics Project. The members of Nuffield Foundation believed that children were learning to hate mathematics because of senseless drill that dulled their taste for learning. They proceeded to set up experimental programs using a laboratory method. Participants in these programs were students who ranged in ages from 5 to 13.

Characteristics of the Nuffield Mathematics Project

1. Children cannot learn abstract mathematical concepts in their early years without relating them to real objects. Emphasis is placed on using seeds, rocks, blocks, scales, measuring devices, etc. Today these are called manipulatives.

2. Each child proceeds at his/her own pace. This means that not all the children will be learning the same math skills at the same time. Individualization is stressed.

3. Active learning is emphasized over lecture and drill. Children interact with a rich, varied environment in the classroom to make their own mathematical discoveries. Mathematical understanding is gained through experience with real-life objects.

4. Attending to the interests of students is necessary for understanding, and learning situations are set up to foster the eager interaction of the child with the materials. For example: The classroom contains centers with activities, such as working in the toy store, cooking with real food, and making things by measuring and cutting. In many cases, math will naturally grow out of play experiences during these activities.

5. It is essential to include teaching situations that may be considered unmathematical in order to develop mathematical sense relevant to the real world. Today these methods might be called teaching across the curriculum.

6. Material for problems and study can also be taken from children's literature like *The Three Little Pigs* (TCM 551) and *Goldilocks and the Three Bears* (TCM 550). Today this activity would be considered a math-literature connection.

7. Instead of doing worksheets, students should record their work by making graphs, designing displays, drawing pictures, and writing about their mathematics projects.

8. Students should create many of the math experiences, but the teacher is an active guide and participant. Emphasis is on having students understand how to learn and think for themselves.

Many of these ideas may sound familiar. They are over thirty years old.

Changing Math Instruction (cont.)

Effective Math Instruction Varies

Multi-age classrooms handle math instruction with a variety of methods. Some classrooms will have a K-2 structure or another combination. Some teachers may be working in multi-age classes for the first time, while others may be very experienced. It takes time for new teachers to assemble idea books and materials. There will be many differences from school to school and from class to class. Teaching will become easier as more texts and curriculums are written specifically for multi-age classes. Schools will need to spend more on materials.

The Whole-Class Approach

This method works best in classrooms that combine grades one and two. Compare the teacher guides for first and second grade math. In most cases, you will find that they are practically identical. For example, in the introduction section of *Explorations in Math* (Addison-Wesley, 1993) the scope and sequence of grades one and two are compared side by side on pages vii, viii, and ix. The main difference is that the second grade problems use greater numbers. It is often possible to teach both grade levels together as a large group. Just change the numbers in the problems. In one example, you could use single-digit numbers and in the next problem use two-or three-digit numbers. Many teachers choose this method for the first year of multi-age teaching.

Whole-class instruction should be precise and brief. After a quick large-group lesson, students move into groups or centers to work with manipulatives, record math concepts, and complete evaluations. Then you can move from group to group, tutor individuals, or call students to small group instruction in flexible groups. This is the same format used in the language arts block.

Team Teaching

In another school a similar method may be used but with a different structure. The classrooms in this example have three different age groups, K–2. Teachers each have a team teaching partner for the math hour only. A topic such as money is chosen, and students are flexibly grouped according to mathematical needs. Students are grouped across grade levels so that each may proceed at his/her own pace. One teacher takes the group needing more concrete experiences, while the other works with students who need more abstract activities. Student needs are assessed by a test given at the beginning of the year and again by a pre-test given before each unit.

When the teachers begin another topic, such as telling time, students are regrouped by a pre-test. This method results in a more precise match of instruction to student needs. It also ensures that students who are ready to move on are able to do so. As a result, those with superior ability get the benefit of an accelerated curriculum. This structure is similar to ability grouping and simple exchange; however, there are differences. Students are coming from a multi-age setting, and placement is determined by instructional need, not age. Groups are not static, and students are freed from the barriers of grade-level placements. There is constant regrouping, if necessary, as each topic is introduced. It is not unusual for a first grader to consistently work at a second grade math level.

Changing Math Instruction (cont.)

Small Groups and Centers

This method is suitable for any combination of ages. For this type of instruction, students stay in their own classroom. The teacher works with one or two small instructional groups each day, while the other children work in Math Centers. (See pages 95–113 for more information about Math Centers.) Groups are flexible to meet each learner's needs. After the math groups, the teacher monitors and evaluates the activities in Math Centers, gives tests, and conferences with students. Emphasis is on individualization. Instruction is shifted from the old method (large-group instruction, demonstration, and completion of workbook pages) to a laboratory method. Several changes are sometimes necessary for this method to work effectively:

1. Be sure to do consistent evaluations and observations with each student on a weekly basis.

2. Centers must be designed so that students can learn directly from the materials without constant teacher intervention or supervision.

3. The computer can help students learn math skills. Select programs that do some assessment while enabling students to progress at their own rates. Computers are more effective with students who are ready for abstract mathematical experiences, but it also reinforces concepts and provides practice for students at all levels.

4. Every effort must be made to expand mathematics instruction by using math related literature for reading instruction and during read aloud and silent reading times. The small group method may be combined with the whole class approach on page 55.

Some Characteristics of the Laboratory Method

- Use of manipulatives
- Small groups or individuals
- Use of student discovery
- Use of math centers
- Weekly or daily math challenge/bonus question

- Emphasis on problem solving, rather than computation
- Cooperative learning in mathematics
- Students write about math or create problems
- Connect literature to mathematics
- Use of math centers

Notice that these characteristics are not exclusive to the multi-age classroom. In fact, many teachers in the United States began using these methods with the publication of Mary Baratta-Lorton's *Mathematics Their Way* (Addison-Wesley, 1976). See page 54 to read about the Nuffield Mathematics Project. A big step forward in mathematics education was the introduction of manipulatives, such as interlocking cubes and colored rods of different lengths.

First Steps

Teachers just beginning to implement the laboratory method, or multi-age math instruction, should not be expected to use traditional tests or curriculums. While such materials can be adapted for multi-age use, it is time consuming. Teachers need to concentrate their efforts on collecting materials and planning lessons. There is no time for them to write instructional guides. Administrators should make it a top priority to provide all the necessary instructional materials and manipulatives.

Changing Math Instruction (cont.)

Instructional Guides—Some Old, Some New

- *Mathematics Their Way* by Mary Baratta-Lorton (Addison-Wesley, 1993)–Note the special planning guides on pages 366-384. There is also a glossary of materials on page 360. There is a series of books by Mary Baratta-Lorton that may also be helpful such as *Workjobs* and *Workjobs II* (Addison-Wesley, 1987–1988).

- *Explorations in Math* by B. Coombs, L. Harcourt, J. Travis, and N. Wannamaker (Addison-Wesley, 1993) — This series of texts uses the same philosophy as *Mathematics Their Way.*

- *Math in Stride* by C. Clark, B. Carter, and B. Sternberg (Addison-Wesley, 1993) — This manipulative-based series is designed for grades 1–6 and has an excellent appendix of diagnostic tasks for evaluation.

- *Developing Number Concepts Using Unifix Cubes* by Kathy Richardson (Addison-Wesley, 1984) — This book covers kindergarten through third grade and provides good activities for small group instruction.

- *Connecting Math and Literature* by John and Patty Caratello (Teacher Created Materials, 1991) —This is an excellent resource for the primary grades.

- *Box It or Bag It Mathematics* by Burk, Snider, and Symonds (The Math Learning Center, Bassett Press, 1988).—This material works best for first and second grade combinations.

- *I Do and I Understand* from the Nuffield Foundation (John Wiley & Sons, 1967) — In the same year, the Nuffield Foundation published three other teacher guides: *Mathematics Begins, Pictoral Representation,* and *Beginnings.* Because of their age, these books may be difficult to locate.

- *Early Childhood Units for Math* by Sandra Merrick (Teacher Created Materials, 1993) — The last three chapters introduce operations through literature and patterns.

Mathematics Help

When you join the National Council of Teachers of Mathematics, you will receive a magazine called *The Arithmetic Teacher* which is a source of help and inspiration. Each issue is like a college mini-course. In addition to many excellent publications, this organization has extremely helpful programs and conferences through state and local related organizations. Some of the state conferences are too good to miss.

National Council of Teachers of Mathematics

1906 Association Drive

Reston, VA 22091-1593

Math Literature

The Importance of Math Literature

One of the highest priorities for the classroom library should be a permanent collection of math-related literature. Extensive use of such literature gives math instruction energy and reality while generating excitement. True math enrichment cannot occur without cross-curricular activities and the imaginative correlation of literature. Quality is just as important as quantity, so the books should be carefully selected. Ask librarians and fellow teachers to suggest their favorite math literature. Then consult the bibliographies in math teacher resource books.

A Time Bonus

Most teachers have trouble getting everything done during the instructional day. Using math-related literature may save you enough time to teach an extra group, tutor a child, or catch up on classroom observations. Simply choose a book such as *Alexander Who Used to Be Rich Last Sunday* by Judith Viorst (Aladdin, 1988). One or two groups can use it for reading, and the whole class can use it for math. Be sure to plan appropriate math activities for each math level. Simple money skills like identifying coins and bills can be taught to young children. Coin values and operations with money can be used for older students. Most students are probably ready to understand that there are several ways to make a dollar: 4 quarters, 2 half dollars, 100 pennies, etc. Also, the whole class will enjoy estimating what they can buy with a dollar. This would be an excellent time to set up a toy store in the Home/Dramatic Play Center. Look for additional money experiences on pages 103–104. Second graders and some first graders will be able to write about additional Alexander books in their reading logs. Another Alexander favorite is *Alexander and the Terrible, Horrible, No Good, Very Bad Day* by Judith Viorst (Atheneum, 1972).

Repetition

Some teachers are concerned that if the same books are repeated year after year, students will become bored and disinterested. Math-related literature does need to be repeated but perhaps not every year. If the unit built around the Alexander stories is repeated every other year, a few children will hear it twice, and some will hear it only once. There will be a two-year space between readings. By that time many children will not remember the book at all. Children actually enjoy repetition and ask for it. A seven-year-old will have a different perspective than he/she did as a five-year-old. The repeated math unit will require a different set of skills than it did two years earlier. So some repetition of math literature and math instruction is desirable and even necessary in multi-age classrooms.

Math Literature (cont.)

The Math Research Center

The Math Research Center can be divided into three areas: (1) computers, (2) math puzzles, games, and math literature, (3) math tapes for the listening area. See Using Technology (pages 120–123) for suggested math software. You may have to make your own tapes to go with the math books. Be sure to get some Hap Palmer math tapes for the listening area.

Suggestions for the Math Literature Shelf

Aylesworth, Jim. *The Completed Hickory Dickory Dock.* Atheneum, 1990.

Backer, John Leonard. *Seven Little Rabbits.* Scholastic, 1973.

Bang, Molly. *Ten, Nine, Eight.* Greenwillow, 1983.

Carle, Eric. *1 2 3 to the Zoo.* Philomel, 1968.

Carle, Eric. *The Grouchy Ladybug.* Harper & Row, 1986.

Carle, Eric. *The Secret Birthday Message.* Harper & Row, 1986.

Carle, Eric. *The Very Hungry Caterpillar.* Putnam, 1981.

Carter, David A. *How Many Bugs in a Box?* Simon & Schuster, 1988.

Crews, Donald. *Ten Black Dots.* Morrow, 1986.

Ehlert, Lois. *Fish Eyes.* Harcourt, Brace, Jovanovich, 1990.

Feelings, Muriel. *Moja Means One.* Dial, 1971.

Gag, Wanda. *Millions of Cats.* Putnam, 1977.

Hulme, Joy. *Sea Squares.* Disney, 1991.

Hutchins, Pat. *The Doorbell Rang.* Mulberry, 1986.

Lionni, Leo. *A Busy Year.* Scholastic, 1992.

Lionni, Leo. *Inch by Inch.* Astor-Honor, 1960.

Mathews, Louise. *Bunches and Bunches of Bunnies.* Scholastic, 1978.

McMillan, Bruce. *Eating Fractions.* Scholastic, 1991.

Peters, Sharon. *Five Little Kittens.* Troll, 1981.

Schwartz, David. *How Much Is a Million?* Scholastic, 1985.

Zolotow, Charlotte. *One Step, Two....* Lothrop, 1981.

This is only a partial list of the math-related literature available. Several titles are available as Big Books, such as *A Busy Year, The Very Hungry Caterpillar, The Doorbell Rang, Ten Black Dots,* etc. In addition to the books already listed, there is a series of math books written by Mitsumasa Anno especially suitable for the Math Research Center. Perhaps the one to start with is *Anno's Math Games* (Philomel, 1982).

Math Anecdotal Record

Student's Name: _____

Grading Period: _____

First Week	Second Week	Third Week
Fourth Week	Fifth Week	Sixth Week

Centers and Megacenters

Centers

The most effective classrooms contain areas where students can interact with materials in a prepared environment. While centers have always been a feature of early childhood classrooms, extensive use of student-initiated activities is new to some primary grades. Expansion of centers into the primary grades was encouraged by Maria Montessori, Mary Baratta-Lorton , the Nuffield Foundation, and others. The classroom is divided into areas that can go by a variety of names, including work stations, learning centers, or centers of interest.

Most teachers have 4–10 centers, depending on the ages of the children and the size of the classroom. The diversity of students, differing classroom sizes, and availability of materials contribute to an infinite variation of classroom learning areas. Using centers for a large part of the day may require a philosophical change on the part of some first and second grade teachers. To begin with, the teacher must feel confident that students can learn from the classroom materials, books, and manipulatives without his/her constant, direct supervision or intervention. Then the teacher must adjust to the idea of teaching new skills, such as learning how to learn, designing one's own learning experiences, developing imagination, understanding relationships, and appreciating and creating beauty. When the students of today become the workers of tomorrow, they will need to be active self-starters, not passive employees waiting for constant instruction.

Megacenters

A megacenter is a grouping of centers offering a variety of activities on different levels. Students sign up for, or are assigned to, the megacenter for a long period of time, usually an hour or more. If a project is finished quickly, there are other enticing activities to fill the time allotted. This prevents students from wandering around the classroom and bothering others. To increase the possibilities at a megacenter, the activities are not limited to the materials in that center. Other supplies are brought into the center as needed.

Planning for Center-Based Instruction

The new structure of multi-age programs requires setting up a classroom plan that enables students to work in depth on self-initiated projects. In other words, students must be able to help themselves and each other. Each center must provide a variety of materials close at hand. Students should have several activities from which to choose. Choice increases motivation. The easiest way to accomplish all this is to make several little mini-centers within each center or to group several centers together into a megacenter.

A Sample Classroom Setup is shown on page 65. Feel free to alter this design to accommodate the needs and interests of your students, to make the best use of your materials and furniture, and to fit the space you have available.

Designing Megacenters

Combinations

To make a megacenter, combine centers by location or topic. For example, the traditional Home Center can be expanded to include a wide variety of activities. Add a box of dress-up materials, and the center is also the Dramatic Play Center. This combination will keep the kindergartners interested for longer periods of time. To assure the interest of the first and second graders, add a puppet theater, puppets, a flannel board and plenty of flannel board figures of storybook characters. Provide a table to write plays for puppets or real characters. Be sure to place different types of colored paper, glue, and  other materials for making costumes nearby or in the center. You may wish to include the room's main library in this center. If not, be sure to place a small storybook library there. Younger children will need plenty of magazines and old catalogues to use for cutting out pictures. First and second graders focus on creating a product, so blank books should be included along with teacher demonstration products and examples of completed student work. There should be plenty of stiff paper or poster board, craft sticks, and other craft materials for students to use when creating puppets or paper dolls to represent the characters in a book.

Other Megacombinations

Math and blocks are a natural combination for a megacenter if they are placed back to back as illustrated on the sample floor plan (page 65).

Art and publishing are a natural combination, as well. In this megacenter, it is possible for students to create a complete book. A student author can do either the illustrations or the text first, depending on his/her learning style. This megacenter should include a table, a bookshelf stocked with art supplies, and some easels. Tabletop easels can be used to save space. In addition, students should have access to a nearby sink to make cleaning up an easier task.

Computers and research go well together. You may also choose to locate the main library in this center instead of the Home/Dramatic Play Center. To provide quiet alternative activities, include puzzles, pegboards, parquetry, and other manipulatives in this megacenter.

A table located between the Research Center and the Reading/Skills Center can serve both centers.

The Theme Center is also the science and social studies center. Time spent in the theme center substitutes for formal science and social studies lessons. See the section about Theme Centers (pages 76–87). The Theme Center is located near the small-group instructional area. This allows students to easily move projects they begin during small-group instruction to the Theme Center for completion.

Designing Megacenters (cont.)

Stocking the Megacenters

All centers should have certain basic materials. Use the following checklist for suggestions on what to stock in your megacenters.

☐ Writing Paper   ☐ Scissors

☐ Construction Paper   ☐ Rulers

☐ Crayons   ☐ Poster Board

☐ Glue   ☐ Old Magazines and Catalogues

Materials, such as paper, crayons, glue, and scissors can be housed in each center, or each student can have supplies in a box that she/he takes from center to center. If the materials cannot be stored directly in each center, they should be placed in a central location that is accessible to all centers.

Most centers will also have a selection of books. It may take time to outfit each center with a sufficient number of appropriate books, but it is worth the effort. Start with books from your school or public library. Then build a personal collection as possible.

Setting Up the Classroom

Maximizing Space

Before making a room plan, try to observe other multi-age classrooms. Visit programs at other schools, if possible. Examine the floor plans of regular kindergarten and preschool classrooms in your own building. In most classes, floor space in classrooms for young children is conserved by placing seats within the centers. Then the centers can be made larger and use more central floor space. You may also wish to save space by using a file cabinet rather than a teacher's desk. Plan an instructional area for reading stories and quick lessons. Children can be seated on the floor for these activities. A corner near a chalkboard usually works best. Be sure to provide a rug for seating if there is no carpet. Place a bookshelf close at hand or a cart with wheels to hold your teaching materials. Another alternative is to organize your teaching materials in plastic totes so that you can access them as needed. Locate the teaching area near an electrical outlet so that you can use equipment such as a tape recorder, filmstrip projector, and overhead projector during instruction. A short easel for Big Books is also helpful to have in the instructional area.

Noise Zones

It is usually helpful to divide the room into quiet and noisy areas. Of course, the noise level will vary, depending on how the centers are used.

Noisy areas:	*Quiet areas:*
Home/Dramatic Play Center	Small Group Instructional Area
Block Center	Multi-Purpose Table
Theme Center (social studies and science activities)	Research/Library Center
Art/Publishing Center	Computer Area
	Math Center
	Publishing Center
	Reading/Skills Center
	Listening/Author Center

One room may not contain all these centers at the same time. The room arrangement is usually limited by features such as doors, windows, chalkboards, outlets, and sinks. The Theme Center, for social studies and science activities, should be located near a sink and, if possible, a window. The Art Center should also be close to a sink. Any area used for small group instruction or individual tutoring should be placed as far away as possible from noisy areas such as the Home/Dramatic Play Center, Block Center, and sink. The computers should be close to the teacher table so that you can monitor their use and correct problems with a minimum of interruption.

Sample Classroom Setup

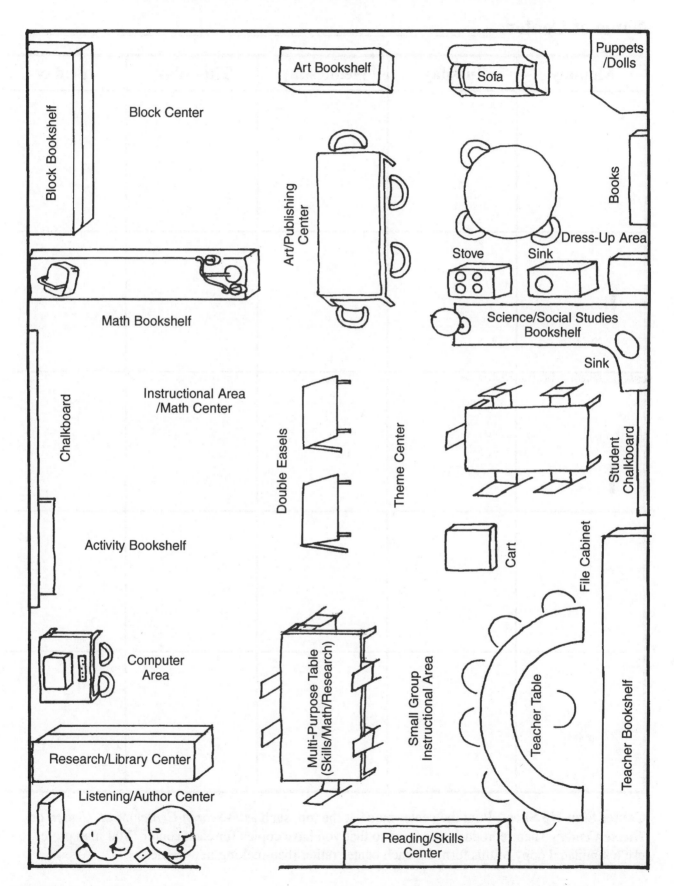

Block Center

Block Bookshelf

Art Bookshelf

Sofa

Puppets /Dolls

Books

Art/Publishing Center

Math Bookshelf

Stove

Sink

Dress-Up Area

Science/Social Studies Bookshelf

Sink

Chalkboard

Instructional Area /Math Center

Double Easels

Theme Center

Student Chalkboard

Activity Bookshelf

Cart

File Cabinet

Computer Area

Multi-Purpose Table (Skills/Math/Research)

Small Group Instructional Area

Teacher Table

Teacher Bookshelf

Research/Library Center

Listening/Author Center

Reading/Skills Center

Center Sign-Up Sheet

Name of Center: _____

Monday	Tuesday	Wednesday	Thursday	Friday

Center Sign-Up Sheet: Print the center name at the top, such as *Research Center, Math Center,* or *Theme Center.* Then reproduce this form so that you have copies for each center. You may prefer to use a laminated copy of this form for each center rather than making new copies.

Choosing Materials

Independent Use of Materials

The ideal material allows the child to learn directly from it with little or no adult supervision or intervention. In this manner, children become active learners, not passive ones. The younger the child, the greater the need for concrete objects. Play must be an integral part of the learning process. For this reason, the primary concern when selecting learning materials should be whether or not a child can use them on his/her own. For example, nesting blocks teach seriation through a discovery method. The material can be placed in the center, and often with no instruction at all, children will stack them. When it is time to clean up, children will seek to return them to their original nesting position. Adults can interact with the children to help them to add to their language skills by using new words and concepts, such as *small-smaller-smallest, large-larger-largest, size,* and *in order.* This is highly preferable to using workbooks in which children glue three bowls in front of the three bears according to their sizes. If a written record is required, children can trace the blocks in order on a large piece of paper and attempt to label them. Related materials, such as rods of different lengths and blocks that make number stairs, are provided in the Math Center. Extend the concept into other centers by putting measuring cups in the Science Theme Center. Have three different-sized, stuffed bears with three different-sized bowls in the Home/Dramatic Play Center. Three different-sized detergent tops serve nicely as the bears' bowls. Have books about sizes, such as *Goldilocks and the Three Bears* and *The Three Billy Goats Gruff,* in the Home/Dramatic Play Center and the Library Center.

In the Art/Publishing Center older children can rewrite these favorites in their own words and add their own illustrations. It is impossible to overestimate the importance of the environment in the multi-age classroom.

Here are some examples of excellent learning materials.

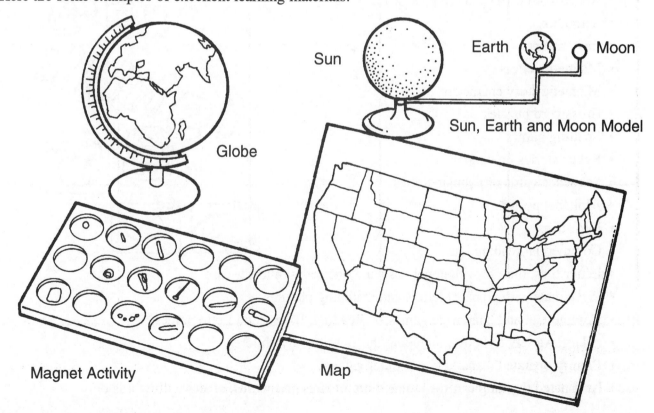

Globe

Sun

Earth   Moon

Sun, Earth and Moon Model

Magnet Activity

Map

Reading Center

This is the center where the children like to play school. Usually they will start to play school spontaneously, and you can add desks, small chalkboards, charts, pointers, big books, and instructional materials. If the children have not played school by midterm, model the activity and set up the school in January.

For the younger children, especially kindergartners, emphasis should be on concrete materials and on process. For the older children, recording activities and products become more important. Kindergartners may join the older children in completing a product if they wish, since they will be working at the same center, but they should not be forced to do so. Do not expect kindergartners to complete a product each time they go to a center. This would force an early emphasis on the abstract and not allow enough developmental time at the concrete level.

Equipment for the Reading Center

- Chalkboard, chalk, and erasers
- Large magnetic board or metal file cabinet
- Bookshelf or book display
- Stapler
- Shelves
- Typewriter(s)

Materials for the Reading Center

- Word cards, at least one set with pictures
- Alphabet blocks
- Teacher-made blank booklets
- Blank word cards and sentence strips
- Scrap box
- Easy readers
- Magnetic letters
- Magnetic story characters
- Crossword puzzles
- Spelling games
- Rebus stories on charts
- Sequence cards of popular stories
- Alphabet poster
- Filmstrips
- Commercial reading kits
- Letter tiles, one set with upper-case and one set with lower-case
- Place mats with alphabet letters and matching pictures
- Commercial and handmade games — Reading, Bingo, and Lotto games
- A large variety of books, including those written by children
- Battery operated, hand-held computer games
- Laminated rhyming cards — some with pictures and words, others with words only

Skills Center

What Is a Skills Center?

Although the main emphasis in reading has shifted away from acquiring isolated skills, students still need some practice in areas like alphabet recognition, phonics, and reading comprehension. Instead of practicing in a workbook, students now learn skills in relation to the literature they are studying. Workbooks can also be replaced by manipulatives and games that foster learning. These can be packaged in small see-through containers and/or plastic bags and placed in the Skills Center. Each packet serves one or two students. Often children work in pairs since it encourages vocabulary development and verbalization of learning strategies.

Matching Center Materials to Test Objectives

1. **Objective:** Use antonyms as clues to the meanings of new words.

   Skill Packet: Provide opposite cards to match.

2. **Objective:** Arrange events in sequential order.

   Skill Packet: Arrange picture cards or sentences in order.

3. **Objective:** Describe the setting of a story.

   Skill Packet: Furnish writing materials and pictures of places from magazines or small study prints. Each student chooses a picture and writes a short description. If possible, staple the picture to the student's work.

4. **Objective:** Identify cause-and-effect relationships.

   Skill Packet: Supply cause-and-effect cards. Some children can simply match the cards, and others can write about the cause and effect.

5. **Objective:** Understand the feelings and emotions of characters.

   Skill Packet: Match the drawings of facial emotions to the drawings of related situations.

   Example: Match a picture of a birthday cake and presents to a picture of a child's happy face. Look at literature being read to get some ideas for pictures that show emotions. The birthday pictures described above could be used after reading the book *Mop Top* by Don Freeman (Viking, 1955). Another example would be to match a scared face to an alligator under a bed after reading *There's an Alligator Under My Bed* by Mercer Mayer (Dial, 1987). You may wish to have older students match a sentence to each face.

6. **Objective:** Distinguish between fact and nonfact.

   Skill Packet: Sort real and make-believe cards. Younger students can sort cards that have pictures, and the older students can sort cards with real and make-believe sentences.

7. **Objective:** Identify the beginning sounds of words.

   Skill Packet: Match plastic letters to pictures of objects.

Educational catalogues are packed with excellent materials. Examples include: *Three Bear Family Counters* (Teacher Created Materials) and *What Am I? Riddle Cards* (Educational Insights).

Listening Center

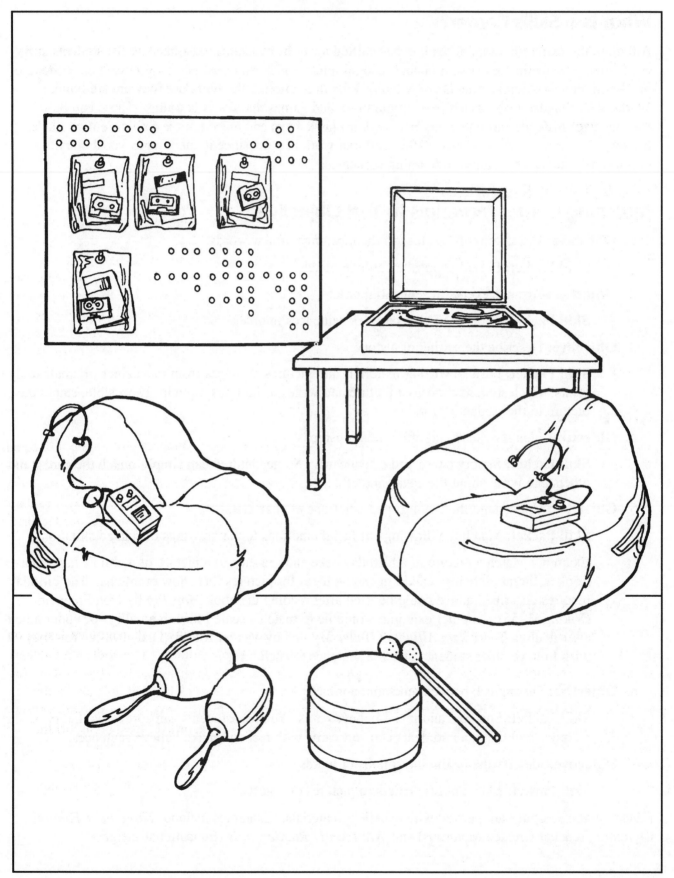

Listening Center (cont.)

Stepping into Literacy

A Listening Center may be the most important center in the room. Seize every opportunity to acquire books with tapes that match. It is best to have at least two copies of the book to go with each tape. Work toward obtaining multiple copies of the very best books. Usually a Listening Center can be combined with an Author and/or Music Center to make a megacenter. Plastic reclosable bags can be used to display books and tapes together. The opportunity to hear stories read aloud is essential for literacy.

The Value of Repetition

Given the opportunity, most children will repeatedly request to hear the same books read. Many different forces can interfere with parents reading to their children at the home: poverty, television, shift work, working mothers, and much more. Some children come to school without the listening experiences that are so essential for reading success. While such deficiencies are difficult to overcome, a library of tapes will go a long way to remediate the problem. Students can listen to the same tapes over and over while following along in the books. Working in pairs seems to stimulate learning as children assist each other and share the experience. Students like to memorize books and read along, an important first step to literacy. Blank tapes can be provided so fluent readers can make tapes to add more stories to the library in the Listening Center.

Motivation

If a book or a tape is added to the center with no mention of preparation, students will not be interested. Before a book and tape set are placed in the center, the book should be read aloud with a great deal of excitement and affection. If there are magnetic board characters, dolls, or activities to go with the story, children will listen to it again and again. Use the shared-reading or after-lunch-read-aloud time to build motivation. Occasionally, plan an art reading response for the whole class. Have students use tempera paint, watercolors, or markers to create their pictures. Play the tape aloud in the background as the artists create.

Training Is Important

Training students how to use the equipment in the Listening Center is essential. Plan a quick lesson on how to use the tape recorder and headphones. Make a list of the major points to repeat during damage control time on another day. Try to find a tape recorder that is especially designed for student use. In other words, be sure that it is sturdy and easy to use. You may wish to stick colored dots above the buttons on the recorder to help nonreaders. Use green for play, red for stop, orange for rewind, yellow for pause, and blue for fast forward. To prevent students from erasing recorded tapes, break off the little tabs on the backs of the cassettes. If, at a later time, you decide to record over a tape, just cover the holes in the back of the cassette with transparent or masking tape. Tapes do sometimes break, however, so be sure to make back-up copies. An alternative is to use a tape player instead of a tape recorder.

Listening Center (cont.)

Choosing Equipment

When selecting tape recorders, keep in mind that students usually do not like to work alone. Recorders with two ports for headphone jacks are a good choice. Pairs of students working together can listen to the same tape. Another choice is to pick a user-friendly tape recorder, such as those made by Fisher Price, and not use headphones. This is an especially good idea if the class includes kindergartners because they are sometimes rough on tape recorders. Some teachers cannot tolerate extra noise, but listening without earphones is often a good idea if the volume is kept at a reasonable level. There is the added advantage that other students can hear the story or music while they work in an adjacent center. It doubles the educational benefit and is actually similar to the way children learn at home, listening to the radio or TV while they play.

The Hidden Benefits of Music

In addition to music tapes or CD's, students can also learn to read by listening to songs. Make or buy a set of charts with words to familiar songs. Provide a blunt stick, such as a ruler, for a pointer. Children can read and/or sing along at the same time. Some research has indicated that this is an excellent method of instruction for students who need additional help with reading. An alternative would be to place laminated copies of song lyrics in a class scrapbook which is kept in the Listening Center. Be sure that each page has colorful drawings to stimulate interest. These can be provided by students working in the Art Center. It helps to enlarge the print of the lyrics and to make them as dark and bold as possible.

Special Tapes

Some children need to have the materials modified in order to be successful. Tapes often move too fast for beginners to match spoken words with the printed ones. You can choose some easy books and record them while reading at a much slower pace. To get some idea of the correct oral reading tempo, touch each word of the text with your finger as you record the story. Encourage students to follow along in the book by pointing to each word as it is read.

Where to Begin

Student interest is the most important factor to consider when choosing books and tapes. Dr. Seuss stories should be the first acquisitions for your Listening Center. Always try to have two books to match each tape. The easiest Dr. Seuss books are *Hop on Pop* (Random, 1963) and *Green Eggs and Ham* (Random, 1960). Scholastic and Troll Book Clubs usually have a good selection of matching books and tapes.

Listening Center (cont.)

A Sendak Reference Book

If you wish to get an inside picture of how a great author and artist works, try to purchase or check out *The Art of Maurice Sendak* by Selma G. Lanes (Harry N. Abrams, 1993). Although this book is too expensive and heavy for children to handle by themselves, take time to share the pictures and information with students. It also contains an excellent bibliography of Sendak's books.

Research Center

Basic Materials

Thanks to CD-ROM technology, every classroom can now have an encyclopedia. This is why the computers should be located in or adjacent to the Research Center. There should also be an encyclopedia in book form for cross-reference or for browsing. There should also be a selection of dictionaries, including picture dictionaries. The school library will probably have a variety of easy dictionaries. Bring several types to the classroom to review. Then have students try them out and carefully observe when they are using the dictionaries. Different dictionaries can vary greatly in quality, and you will want to be very discriminating as to which ones you buy or check out for your classroom. Sometimes the library will have extra sets of *Childcraft* that can be checked out

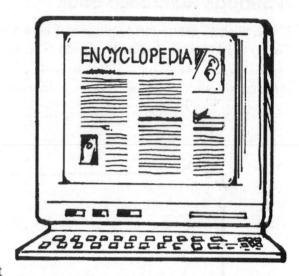

for use in the classroom. The same is true for out-of-date encyclopedias. Of course, it would be preferable to have all new reference materials, but this is seldom possible because of the expense involved. Usually the CD-ROM encyclopedia will be the most up-to-date. Students should be made aware of the importance of current information when doing their research.

Beyond Basic Materials

As each theme is introduced, you will notice that students show more interest in some books than in others. Day after day, they may choose the same books during open time. Students who are especially interested in a book will often copy illustrations or even the text. Popular books should stay in the Research Center even after the thematic unit is completed. It is helpful to place a removable colored coding dot on the spines and then place the books for a specific theme in a magazine holder. On your list of thematic materials, place a star beside the books that prompted sustained student interest. Keep these in the classroom for an additional month or two until interest begins to wane. If you have any funds that are allocated for your classroom, use the money to make these books permanent additions to your library. An excellent choice for the classroom library would be some of the Eyewitness Books Series published by Alfred A. Knopf in 1989. For example, some books that would be good to use with a water unit include: *Shell, Seashore, Whale, Pond and River, Amphibian, Fish, Shark,* and *Boat.* The text is intended for students in the intermediate or higher grades. However, younger students will find that a great deal of information can be obtained from the stunning illustrations and photographs. Even a five-year-old would be captivated by pictures that look like a visit to a museum or an aquarium. You may wish to ask a parent volunteer to make some tapes to go with the texts. Some additional titles that interest primary children are *Birds, Butterfly and Moth, Car, Cowboy, Desert, Dinosaur, Dog, Elephant, Fossil, Horse, Insect, Mammal, Plant, Rocks and Minerals, Sports, Tree, Volcano and Earthquake,* and *Weather.* There are too many to list. Another series to borrow from the library is the *New True Books Series* published by Childrens Press.

Research Center (cont.)

Suggested Magazines

Ranger Rick is an outstanding magazine for primary children. It has great nature photos, and it is all about animals and natural history. (ages 6–12)

Zoobooks is actually a series of books. They have animal facts with terrific photos and art. Each issue is about one subject, such as dolphins or elephants. (ages 7–14)

Kids Discover is a science–oriented magazine. It also focuses on just one subject, such as volcanoes or weather, in each issue. (Ages 6–12)

Kid City is about sports, interesting kids, and hot topics. (ages 6–10)

Barbie is an entertainment magazine for girls. It has projects, adventures, and crafts. (ages 4–8)

Disney Adventures features the Disney characters. There are informational articles about travel, music, and Disney movies and entertainment. (ages 6–14)

Spider is a magazine of stories, comics, and puzzles. (ages 6–9)

Crayola Kids (ages 3-8) or *Pack-O-Fun* (ages 6–12) can be used to give students ideas for projects.

Family PC may be of as much interest to you as it is to students. There are a variety of stimulating ideas to use on the classroom computer, including computer crafts. This may be the intellectual challenge you are looking for. (ages 6–adult)

Go to the library for some back copies of these magazines: *Your Big Backyard, Chickadee, Ladybug,* and *Sesame Street.* They are recommended for younger children but provide easy independent reading for reluctant readers.

You may wish to ask parents to donate discarded magazines that would be appropriate for students to use in the classroom.

Research Cards

Buy these commercially or prepare your own. Provide several levels of difficulty. For the simplest level, use stickers to make research cards for nonreaders. Stickers like dinosaurs, animals, and Mother Goose work especially well. Teacher Created Materials has stickers coordinated with theme materials. By making your own research cards, you can tailor the topics to the resource books that are available in your classroom.

Planning Themes

How to Begin

Start with topics from your local and state curriculums. Then study the suggested center materials for science (pages 85–86) and social studies (page 81) that are listed in this book. Use the Calendar for Planning Themes (page 77) to pencil in some of the suggested topics. Plan opportunities for students to learn how to use special equipment, such as microscopes, globes, scales, magnets, and telescopes. Make a note of equipment related to each theme on the planning calendar. Then start collecting materials and books. A favorite nonfiction book is usually the focal point of each theme. You will need at least two boxes: a small box that is about the same length and width of a pizza box and a large box that is about the size of a copier paper box. If you decide to purchase a large box, it is best to get one that is transparent plastic. The small box will be used for papers, felt figures, teacher guides, and books. As materials are added to the box, make a list of them and tape it inside the box lid. Also, be sure to include a bibliography. The big box is for toys, models, manipulatives, and other large equipment or materials.

Themes Across the Curriculum

You may already realize that themes are just expanded units. All teachers have had training in planning units. The only difference is that themes extend into other subjects, such as reading, art, and math. The following steps will help you prepare a thematic unit.

1. Start with a broad topic, such as water or oceans, that will be your theme.

2. Choose a nonfiction science or social studies book for students to read.

3. Set up the Theme Center with a variety of materials, activities, and books that are related to the theme you have chosen.

4. Plan an art activity related to the theme.

5. Read additional books during read-aloud.

Notice that the topic has already moved from science to reading, language arts, and art. The next step would be a math activity. However, adding math to a thematic unit can be a little harder. As a result, you might decide to wait another year before correlating math skills with your themes. Remember, there is no need to do everything at once. It is easy to get overwhelmed.

Sometimes students can help by writing math problems that go with a theme.

Where to Find Help

The quickest way to plan is to use thematic unit guides. For example, if students are learning about oceans, you could use *Sea Animals* (TCM 254) and *Tide Pools and Coral Reefs* (TCM 249). Try to connect topics such as pollution, our world, rain forests, jungles, and map skills and combine them into one theme, such as ecology. Another source of help is the literature-based series. Examples include: *Connecting Math and Literature* (TCM 243), *Connecting Science and Literature* (TCM 341), and *Connecting Social Studies and Literature* (TCM 345).

Calendar for Planning Themes

YEAR	August	September	October
	November	December	January
	February	March	April
	May	June	July

Make three copies of this planner. Above the word *YEAR,* write **FIRST** on one copy, **SECOND** on another copy, and **THIRD** on the last copy in order to plan your themes for the next three years. Place the pages in a folder or tape them together to create one large planner. Use pencil to fill in the theme(s) for each month. You may wish to plan an alternative theme for each month.

Also plan to use special equipment, such as microscopes, magnets, magnifiers, calculators, scales, telescopes, tape recorders, computers, staplers, and hole punchers.

Using Theme Centers

How to Find Time to Teach Science and Social Studies

A well-planned Theme Center, such as the one illustrated on page 87, will do a great deal of teaching for you. The job of the teacher is changing. Teachers are no longer people who stand in front of the class and impart knowledge by talking and talking. Teachers are becoming guides who help students learn from their environment. As teachers move from center to center, they can interact with students to find out what is being learned. This interaction should not be done like a quiz but should sound like a friendly conversation. Example: *What have you been working on this morning? Have you looked at any of the books? Which one did you like the best? Why? Which toy are you playing with? Did you know there is a toy to match this story? Do you know what it is called? Did you learn something about a manatee?*

Using Science and Social Studies Books as Readers

When the theme is also a science or social studies topic, there is economy of instruction. Even more time is saved if the "reader" is a science or social studies related book. Reading nonfiction approximates real life. People do not read "reading"; they read about something. As a result, reading is given a purpose — to find out about a topic. Students are curious about many real things: rocks, volcanoes, Native Americans, other parts of the world, etc. Many young readers will enjoy the Eric Carle books, and Tomie dePaola writes many nonfiction books that are suitable for older readers.

Using Nonfiction Simplifies Evaluation

During a whole class session, take dictation for the students about the topic being studied and make a fact chart. If you pencil in the initials of the student offering the fact, the chart can be used later for evaluation. Add difficult words to the theme word chart. After the dictation is finished students can write nonfiction books by paraphrasing the chart and adding illustrations. Some children will only be able to draw pictures and copy labels. These activities will provide the teacher with an accurate evaluation of the skills and information being acquired by the students. Use the read-aloud period to present related books that may be too difficult for the student to read alone.

Using Themes Can Be Easy

Themes are carried over into as many subject areas as possible. This is why the materials in the Theme Center should be regarded as portable. Students working in other centers may make short visits to the Theme Center to get materials. The following two rules must be maintained when students wish to borrow materials from the Theme Center:

1. Before borrowing any materials, students from the other centers should ask the children who are working in the Theme Center if those materials are being used.

2. Materials must be returned to the Theme Center during clean-up time.

Using Theme Centers (cont.)

Suggested Themes

Science	Social Studies
Dinosaurs	Community
Rocks	Africa
Plants	Mexico
Water	The Arctic
Space	The Orient
Animal Classification	Native Americans
Magnetism, Energy, and Changes	Maps and Globes

Each of these themes can easily be made into across the curriculum experiences. First, the children explore the Theme Center. This is considered to be a social studies experience. Extend the study into language arts by reading books about the theme. Then, choose a book for the children to read. Continue the theme study by reading several fiction and nonfiction books to the class. Be sure to include chapter books. Choices can be broad; look for related themes. If your social studies topic is the Arctic, look for books on similar topics, such as winter or people of the north. Consider expanding the theme to include the Antarctic and penguins.

More Theme Ideas

Fantasy	Family
Everyday Magic	Cartoons and Comic Strips
Insects	Fairy Tales
Big and Little	Wild Things
That's Impossible (science)	State Symbols
Poetry	Colors
Nursery Rhymes	Circus
Birds	When Horses Were Cars (long ago)
Patriotism and Presidents	Art and Beauty
Animal Homes (habitats)	Nature (classify, compare, make patterns)
Friends	Let's Go (transportation, geography)
Food Around the World	Down Under (Australia)
Seasons and Celebrations	Dr. Seuss
Cultures of the World	Let's Play

Using Theme Centers (cont.)

Making Connections

All the relationships that are apparent to adults must be taught to children. Connections are easy for students if they are taught to look for them. A few simple adjustments in the curriculum can sometimes yield big dividends. For example, a teacher can plan three units, such as oceans, ecology, and rain forests. By sequencing these units as a trio, the teacher can emphasize relationships and generalizations. Pointing out connections results in a much higher level of learning than simply studying rain forests in isolation. Another strategy is to study relationships within the theme. Topics can be broad to include several related subtopics. For example: A theme entitled, "The Earth Long Ago" can include dinosaurs, fossils, rocks, oil, ancient plant life, pre-history, etc. All these subjects are made more meaningful to the student by their connections to each other.

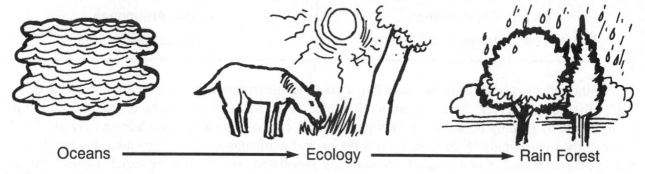

Oceans ⟶ Ecology ⟶ Rain Forest

Changing Themes

Theme Centers can be left up for about four to six weeks. This allows a theme to be experienced in depth and gives the teacher time to collect the necessary materials. The Theme Center is the only center that is always changed each month or grading period. Other centers should be changed, but the changes are gradual and do not take place according to a timetable.

Extending Themes Throughout the Curriculum

As each theme is completed, you may wish to retain some of the exhibits, books, and equipment. These can be incorporated into other centers. Perhaps a tank of fish can be moved to the Art/Publishing Center. Seashells placed in the Art/Publishing Center might inspire a poem after they served as research material for a report some students were working on in the Theme Center. Shells are always popular for stimulating art projects, too. Sometimes students enjoy space themes so much they want to keep some of the space books in the classroom after the unit is finished. Simply move a few of their favorite books into a special space section in the Research Center. If you do not have a Research Center, the space books can move to a new home in the Library Center. The space shuttle and other space toys might be moved to the Block Center where children can use them to design a space city. Space toys would also be appropriately placed in the Art/Publishing Center. Another way to recycle equipment is to create a temporary or special center. When float-and-sink materials have had their turn in the Theme Center, they can move to a Water/Sand Center. Some highly interactive centers, such as small blocks, woodwork, sand, water, painting, music, etc., may have to appear on a rotational basis if there is a limited amount of space in the multi-age classroom. These special centers are essential to the development of kindergarten children, but they also serve a purpose for older children. Contrast time spent in these centers with the hours older children used to spend confined to a desk completing workbook pages. Certainly, interactive centers are to be preferred.

Social Studies Theme Centers

The Importance of Social Studies

Social studies is gaining importance in the primary grades. Learning to appreciate other cultures is a high priority as America continues to become more ethnically diverse. Most businesses must now work and compete at the international level. The thousands and thousands of international business travelers from the United States often find themselves at a linguistic disadvantage. Many jobs require a knowledge of two or more languages. These are factors to keep in mind when planning social studies experiences. The global economy is already here. The challenge is to prepare students to work in the unknown world twenty years in the future.

Geography

Recently published newspapers have contained articles about the results of geographical questions asked of the general public. A few adults could not find the United States on a world map. A large number of adults were unable to locate the Pacific Ocean. Only a few adults were able to find the Persian Gulf shortly after the Gulf War. Again, these are things to keep in mind when planning geography experiences. Social studies will begin to teach itself when related to other subjects. With a little planning, children can gain a better understanding of the world around them. Keep a globe in the classroom and refer to it often. On Columbus Day, even the youngest students can use the globe to see where Christopher Columbus and his crews crossed the Atlantic Ocean in three tiny ships. When studying Thanksgiving compare this to a similar route taken by the Pilgrims. Use the globe again when studying zoo animals to indicate where wild gorillas live in Africa, kangaroos live in Australia, etc. Use stuffed animals and toys in the Theme Center to add interest. Fortunately there are many resources being written today that connect literature with related countries.

Materials for the Social Studies Theme Center

- Tape recorder
- Tapes of songs from around the world
- Foreign language tapes — could be teacher-made or purchased
- Materials for making envelopes and stamps
- Stamps from magazine promotions
- Simple stamp album — could be store-bought or teacher made and laminated
- Postage stamps from around the world
- Flags
- Social studies textbooks
- Commercial social studies kits and games

- Posters of children from other lands
- Posters or objects from other countries
- Postcards
- Chalkboard
- Newspapers and magazines
- Maps and globes
- Wood map puzzles
- Toy telephones
- Map outlines without labels
- Library books and study prints about the U.S. and other countries

Social Studies Theme Centers (cont.)

Social Studies Activities

There is a great deal of flexibility as to where you place materials for a social studies theme. Some of the time there may be an advantage to moving these materials to other centers after students have used them in the Theme Center. Spreading the theme around the room creates experiences across the curriculum. Below are a few suggestions for how to use activities for a social studies theme in other centers.

- **Home/Dramatic Play Center** — Students can dress up in costumes from around the world.

- **Theme Center** — Dolls of different ethnic backgrounds wearing a variety of costumes are an excellent addition.

- **Math or Block Center** — Models of community helpers might be shared with the Math or Block Center.

- **Listening Center** — Literature from different cultures may be taped and presented in the Listening Center.

Map of the World

Map of the United States

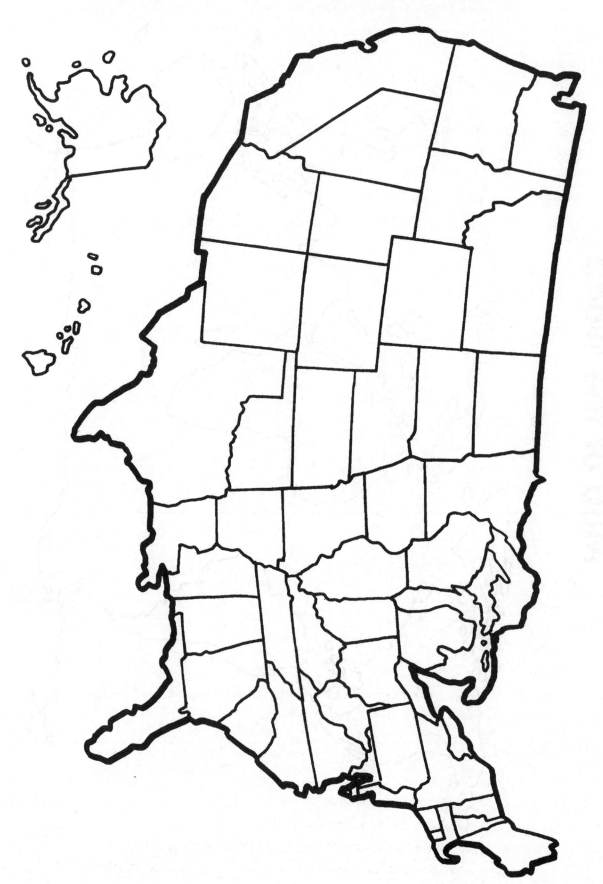

Materials for Science Theme Centers

Related books should be part of every Science Theme Center.

Aquatic Life Displays and Water Experiments

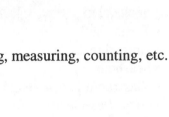

- Large aquarium
- Small plastic containers for minnows, goldfish, or tadpoles
- Materials for float-and-sink experiments
- Dishpans
- Measuring cups and spoons
- Plastic bottles and empty containers of different sizes and shapes plastic lids
- Waterproof aprons
- Small plastic boats; boats made by teacher or students
- Seashell collections — one for display only and another for sorting, measuring, counting, etc.
- Water fun collection — tubes, funnels, bits of wood, etc.
- Bubble-making materials
- Doll clothes and plastic dishes to wash clothesline

Plant Life displays and Experiments

- Different soil samples, including sand and potting soil
- Plastic bags
- Plastic flower pots and other containers, such as egg cartons, empty milk cartons, butter tubs
- Seeds, beans, and collections from fruits and plants
- Small tools for indoor gardening
- Large trays and watering can
- Plastic vases with artificial plants and flowers
- Desert garden
- Terrarium
- Gloves
- Strings
- Interesting plants, such as sweet potatoes or carrot tops
- Observation collection — pine cones, avocado pits, driftwood, bark, tree limbs, twigs, acorns, weeds, cattails, leaves, etc.

Magnetism

- Large horseshoe magnet, wand magnets, bar magnets, rubber magnets, and 8–10 tiny magnets
- Collection of materials to test for magnetic attraction; iron filings
- Small clear plastic container to hold test materials
- Magnetic kits, such as Magnet Discovery Board (manufactured by Lakeshore)
- Magnetic games and activities, such as Magna Doodle (manufactured by Ideal)

Materials for Science
Theme Centers (cont.)

Life Science

- Posters or flannel board pieces of body parts
- Antlers and horns
- Feathers
- Eggshells
- Insects and spider and bug house bug viewer (magnifier)
- Wasp nest or other insect nests honeycomb
- Bird nest (keep in plastic bag)
- Snake skin
- Turtle shell
- Animal teeth
- Seashells
- Classroom pets — earthworms, birds, hamsters, tadpoles, tree hermit crabs, etc.
- Giant flexible zoo animals, farm animals, dinosaurs
- Farm setting
- Microscopes and slides

Process Skills

- Balance scales pan balance
- Plastic or word materials and shapes for sorting
- Animal camouflage cards
- Binoculars
- Kaleidoscope
- Color paddles
- Thermometers
- Prism
- Calendars and clocks
- Mirrors
- Taped animal sounds
- Musical instruments
- Giant magnifier

Earth and Space Science

- Real fossils petrified wood amber
- Rock collection
- Uses for common rock — chalk, salt, coins, flint, etc.
- Pictures of the four seasons
- Toy dinosaurs
- Space toys
- Model showing the relationships of the sun, earth, moon
- Globe world map

Sample Science Theme Center

Water Theme Center

Art/Publishing Center

Book Making Setup

Three elements are needed for the center: a shelf to hold supplies, a table for writing and drawing, and, if possible, easels for painting. In classrooms that include kindergarten through second grade, Art and Publishing Centers are combined to save space. If the classroom combines first and second graders only, there may be space to set up art and publishing as two separate centers.

Create Interest

Some students will be motivated to write and publish with only a suggestion and some blank books. A few will imitate the older students and write book after book, but some will need step-by-step instructions. Begin with books created by the whole class. Choose a topic related to the current theme or to a favorite type of literature. Ask each member of the class to contribute a page or two to the book. Bind the book with yarn, staples, or a binding machine. Be sure to let all the students sign an author page. Display the book in the Art/Publishing Center. As different types of books are completed by students, try to save one of each type for display. There are many teacher resources that suggest different types of books that students can make.

Topics for Student Publishing

- Plants
- Vegetables
- Mother Goose
- Insects
- Under the Sea
- Shapes
- Space
- Let's Play
- The Doctor
- Our Field Trip
- Birds
- My Rock Book
- Snakes and Other

- Pets
- All About Fish
- Comic Book
- My Friends
- My Country
- Sports
- What's in My Closet? (an open door book)
- Fruits
- Favorite Fairy Tales
- Reptiles
- Riddle Book
- Monsters

- Flags
- Dinosaurs
- Around the World
- Leaf Book
- Jungle Animals
- Counting
- Seasons
- Farm
- Holidays
- Make a Pizza
- Favorite Books
- My Country
- Forest Friends

- My Poetry Book
- Weather
- School Days
- All About Me
- Vacation
- Robots
- My Art Work
- Word Book
- Math I Know
- My Dictionary
- Map Book
- Favorite Author Book
- Colors

Art/Publishing Center (cont.)

Small Group Lessons

1. **Magazine Book**

   Distribute old magazines and have students cut out four or five pictures. Glue the pictures to construction paper and staple them into a book. Invite students to make up a story to go with the pictures. Some students will be able to write only one word, while others will be able to write a sentence or paragraph on each page. If students are unable to write a word, the teacher can pencil in a word and for students to trace.

2. **Class Friends Book**

   Begin with several photocopies of each child's photograph. Each child glues the photocopies on paper to make a book of his/her friends. Students pass the books around the group, and each child writes a message to the owner of the book, making this a kind of mini-autograph book. Some children may be able to write only their names beneath their photographs.

3. **Paper doll Book**

   Give students booklets that have about four outlines for paper doll figures. Have them make the figures into characters by drawing faces, hair, and clothing. The paper dolls might become cowboys, storybook people, fashion models, doctor and nurse, family members, etc. Tell students to write about the paper dolls on back of each page.

   • A cowboy wears a hat. He takes care of cows. He rides a horse.

   • Her mother told her not to talk to strangers. She is Little Red Riding Hood.

4. **Cards and Letters**

   Small groups can also write and decorate cards for various holidays, such as Valentine's Day or Mother's Day. They can also write letters to storybook characters, Santa Claus, and real authors.

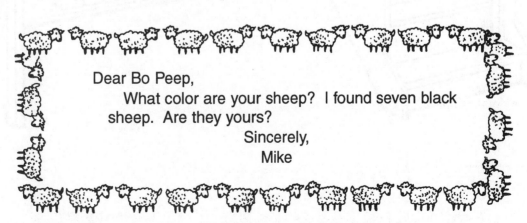

Dear Bo Peep,
   What color are your sheep? I found seven black sheep. Are they yours?
      Sincerely,
      Mike

Library Center

Choosing Books

The room is arranged in centers or work stations. The materials and manipulatives have been carefully prepared. What next? Place books around the classroom and in all of the centers. You will need several types of books:

1. A variety of books for the classroom library

2. Books that are specific to each center

3. Books on a variety of reading levels, from beginner to chapter books

The Library Center shown below includes a loft. This area could also be used as a Dramatic Play Center.

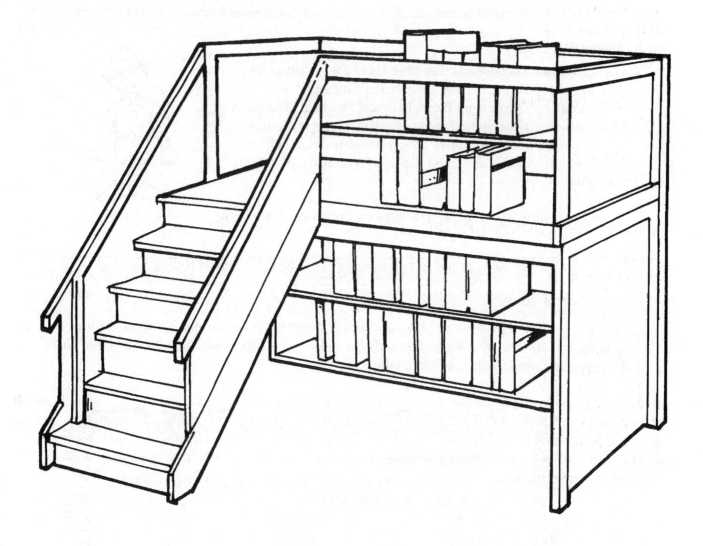

Library Center (cont.)

Combining Centers

The classroom library can be combined with another center to give children a choice of activities. Books should be changed about every four to six weeks. It is very important to try to coordinate book selection with other activities taking place in the room and also with the current season or an upcoming holiday. Be sure to include some easy reader books like Dr. Seuss and the I Can Read series. It is no longer fashionable to use easy readers, but children still like them and want to read them. There are many whole-language companies publishing new easy readers. It is good to have two or more copies of each book.

Where to Place the Books

The Library Center may not have a central location. It may be spread around the room. Books could and should be everywhere. Children will benefit from having books in all of the centers. Some centers will need more books than others. In the K-2 classroom, books from the library may be kept in a center that has the following:

- Storage cubes, bookshelves, or displays for the classroom library
- Quiet manipulatives — puzzles, pegboards, parquetry, etc.
- Plastic bags containing at least two copies of each book with a tape
- Beanbag chairs or other soft furniture
- Literature-related toys

Uses of the Library Center

For the 1–2 classroom, more emphasis is placed on creating products or written production while in the Library Center. As a result, some teachers like to combine the Library Center with the Dramatic Play Center. If these two centers are combined, there should be a puppet stage and materials to make puppets and write plays. Children might also write plays in which they are the characters and create costumes and props for the drama. There should also be a flannel board and felt pieces in the combined Library/Dramatic Play Center. Children can write stories for the flannel board pieces. Be sure to provide a table for students to work at in this center.

In the K–2 classroom a combined Library/Dramatic Play Center must serve a wide range of abilities. It should be a large center and is usually located in a corner to provide walls for the home or store. There are a dining table, a stove, couches, chairs, etc. The theme of this area should be changed each six weeks. Puppets, toys, and a variety of other materials can be used to coordinate with your theme. Suggested themes include:

- Home
- Hospital
- Restaurant
- Store
- Post Office
- Castle or Native American Village

Home/Dramatic Play Center

Home/Dramatic Play Center (cont.)

The New Home/Dramatic Play Center

In years past, the Home/Dramatic Play Center was called the Housekeeping Center, although it served a variety of play scenarios. The new Home/Dramatic Play Center includes everything that the old Housekeeping Center did and more. Plan activities for the Home/Dramatic Play Center and set up props for play. To go beyond teacher-created play, enlist the help of the class when planning for the center. Begin with a favorite piece of literature or with something from the current theme. List the proposed ideas on the chalkboard. Discuss them with students to determine their interest in each topic. This is not like a vote, but if no consensus forms, a vote can be taken. Then discuss the chosen idea to get

suggestions for props and materials from the students. Try to get students to contribute as much as possible. To achieve this, ask yourself the following questions: *Are there materials that can be made by the students themselves, such as masks, headbands, paper bag costumes, or cardboard scenery? Do the students have any materials they can bring from home to share?*

If the ideas proposed by students sound interesting, set up the Home/Dramatic Play Center on a trial basis. The response of the students to the play situation will determine the feasibility of the choice. Some choices will be successful, and some will not sustain students' interests. When you encounter a successful play situation, keep notes of key materials and play experiences for future center topics. It will be two or three years before the chance to use the same subject comes around again. By that time, details will have grown fuzzy without record keeping. While a successful play experience may repeat itself with another class, a new class may have different interests.

Learning from Play

While everyone recognizes the validity of play for kindergartners, some teachers have misgivings about using class time to let older children play. There is good evidence that imaginative play benefits all children in the multi-age classroom. First, a teacher must have some belief that the development of imagination is a worthwhile goal. Younger children have imagination in abundance and are often able to impart spontaneity and learning excitement to older classmates. In turn, the older students contribute their learning experiences and vocabulary to the younger ones. Cooperative learning is essential to obtain the maximum benefits of play. For a more detailed explanation of the validity of multi-age play, read the chapter entitled, "The Little Room" in the book *Full Circle, A New Look at Multi-Age Education* by Penelle Chase and Jane Doan (Heinemann, 1994).

Teachers who are still not convinced that classrooms should devote time to play should try imaginative play experiences on a trial basis. Spend a few minutes each day recording skills or vocabulary arising from play situations. Then make a decision about how to proceed and whether to continue.

Home/Dramatic Play Center (cont.)

Some Ideas for the Home/Dramatic Play Center

- Puppet stage and puppets
- Dishes and flatware
- Costumes from different cultures
- Unbreakable full-length mirror
- Small sofa and chair
- Small kitchen table and chairs
- Play telephones
- Dolls of different ethnic origins wearing traditional costumes
- Cleaning equipment like scrub brushes and brooms
- Cooking utensils like pots and pans
- Dishtowels
- Small rocking chair
- Doll bed
- Kitchen cabinets and sink
- Refrigerator
- Play food
- Range, pot holders, and apron
- Plastic fruits and vegetables
- Magazines and catalogues for cutting
- Old greeting cards

Inexpensive and Free Accessories

Below is a list of suggestions for obtaining inexpensive and free accessories for your Home/Dramatic Play Center.

1. Save empty product boxes from grocery items, such as cereal and rice. If these are opened carefully, they can be glued back together and look as good as new.

2. Open cans, such as those containing soup and green beans, from the bottom instead of the top. Wash them thoroughly and carefully. Then save them for students to use as play food.

3. Ask parents to send outgrown baby clothes that might fit the dolls in the center.

4. Also request old or broken costume jewelry from parents.

5. Wash used plastic butter tubs and similar items. Save them for later use.

6. Look around the house for some old artificial flowers and a plastic vase. Take these to class for the Home/Dramatic Play Center.

7. Have students create play food by drawing, coloring, cutting, and gluing the paper food to cardboard from boxes. You or a parent volunteer can carefully cut out the cardboard foods with a utility knife. Remind students to stay away from the area where the utility knife is being used.

Math Centers

Center-Based Math Instruction

For teachers preparing to begin multi-age instruction, it is best to make changes gradually. Continue with whole-class math instruction at first. Since most multi-age programs do not use workbooks, teachers can begin to move away from dependence on such materials. Do not throw away the workbooks until change can be made without panic. Start by purchasing more manipulatives for the classroom. Concentrate on those materials that can be used without a great deal of teacher supervision or assistance.

- **Step 1:** During morning centers, spend as much time as possible in the Math Center. Observe and make notes to use later. Write down questions and activities that work. Notice any problem areas.

- **Step 2:** Plan a laboratory math period at least one day per week. In the beginning, all students work with the same materials at the same time, for example, counting cubes, pattern blocks, rocks, or buttons. Children can sort, graph, combine sets, or explore permutations. At first, this would be a short 15–20 minute lesson. Use the whole-class method of instruction. Keep careful notes on what worked and what did not. Expand slowly so that half the class is working with one set of manipulatives and the other half is engaged in a different activity. Then prepare four or five areas with different manipulatives or games for each area. Materials for each area could be stored in a specially marked plastic tote or even a cardboard box. Float from area to area with a clipboard, evaluating each activity and planning the next session.

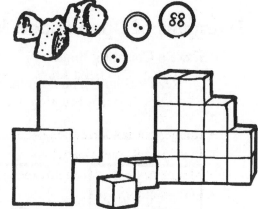

- **Step 3:** To make more time for centers and math labs, combine literature and math during language arts time. Read books about counting and math. Write experience charts and make up math problems as well. The flannel board is very helpful to motivate children's math imaginations. For some excellent suggestions on integrating the curriculum, try *Connecting Math and Literature* by John and Patty Caratello (Teacher Created Materials, 1991).

- **Step 4:** In all of today's classrooms, multi-age and traditional, the emphasis is moving from computational drill to problem solving. Some teachers are confused about what constitutes problem solving. Some ask, "Does it only mean math word problems?" It helps to think of real-life problem solving in all its different facets. Some problem solving is general and includes activities like brainstorming, planning, riddles, organizing projects, and creating or inventing things. Problem solving also has a technical side. Professional problem solvers often need expertise in areas like engineering, math, science, and computer science. (See pages 107–109.)

Math Centers (cont.)

Extending the Quick Math Lesson

General mathematical ideas are presented to the whole class in quick lessons, about 10 minutes each. Of course, time allotment is flexible and can be stretched as long as 20 minutes. Attention must be given to keeping the lesson short so that there will be plenty of time for small groups and centers. It is essential to be prepared for the lesson ahead of time so that it can go quickly. All grade levels are taught together for the quick math lesson. Examples are given for different ability levels. Immediately after the lesson, point out the materials in centers that will extend the lesson. Simple projects that students may wish to do in centers can also be presented at this time. You may wish to read related math literature during the after-lunch-read-aloud time. If students are going to be reading the book themselves, it might be presented during shared reading during the morning. For suggested daily schedule, see Lesson Plans, page 136.

Examples of Open-Ended Math Activities for Centers

1. **Make a Counting Book**

   Read a counting book from the library. Show some teacher-made and student-made counting books. Place a counting display on the flannel board.

   Show some counting toys (such as dominoes) that can be copied by the students. All grade levels can participate in this project at different levels of expectation. Kindergartners can write or glue numerals and draw pictures. First graders and some second graders can make similar books but add some text. Very advanced students can go to the Research Center to study larger numbers. Then they can present a chart, book, or other material to show how to write, read, and represent larger numbers. There are several trade books that deal with large numbers that may be helpful to them in their research. You may wish to show students which counting books would be helpful to them. After that, sit with some kindergarten students to offer help and staple their number books.

   Most of the students should not be required to complete a specific project in the centers, but they must present their work to the class if they choose a different activity from the one suggested.

Math Centers (cont.)

2. Create Patterns

Kindergartners may or may not record their experience in the centers. They can make patterns with cubes, counting animals, felt figures, pegboards, pattern blocks, and other manipulatives. First graders can be encouraged to record their patterns by providing them with pre-cut pattern block shapes, strips of colored paper, graph paper with large squares, fall leaves, etc. It is almost a sure thing that when the younger children see the projects done by the older ones they will try to record their work, too. More advanced levels include progressing to patterns that occur in more than one direction, writing the rules for patterns and discovering patterns in number. Students can write about their projects to explain them. There are chapters on patterns in most of the suggested instructional guides listed on page 57. To keep the youngest children from getting bored, be sure to teach quickly. In addition to linear patterns, show examples of multi-directional patterns, such as a checkerboard, during the quick lesson. After the lesson, discuss number patterns with a small group of advanced students. When finished, visit the centers to observe the recording of patterns or other projects being done by the first graders and kindergartners. Evaluate, using the form on page 98.

3. Explore Geometry and Geoboard Patterns

Begin with simple shapes, such as circles, squares, and triangles. Show how to record geoboard designs on geodot paper (page 99). After the quick lesson, the advanced group can generate some geoboard designs during a small-group session. These can be preserved for use by other students. If you wish to have copies for evaluation, it might be best to make reduced photocopies to save space. Move through other centers, challenging students to create shapes with other manipulatives. Kindergartners can draw, cut, or glue the shapes and then name them. First graders might want to make a shape book and learn how to spell the names of the shapes and then create a shape design for the cover. They can keep a record of the designs they create in their math notebook. Once again, you may wish to reduce the size of the copies to save space.

Converting Workbook Pages to Math Projects

When you feel like providing students with workbook pages, select any math topic and challenge them to create an activity for that skill. It is usually best to model the desired behavior and to show some examples. However, it is also good to talk to the students about the possibilities and leave their options open. After a brief discussion, you might say, "Design a math project. Show us what you have learned about math."

The resulting project will make an excellent addition to most portfolios. If you do not get good results the first time, repeat the assignment. First, do some damage control by asking students to either improve on yesterday's results or choose a new topic. A few students may need some individual instruction to proceed.

Evaluation: Creating Patterns ■○▼

Name: _____ Date: _____

Name: _____ Date: _____

Recording Geoboard Designs

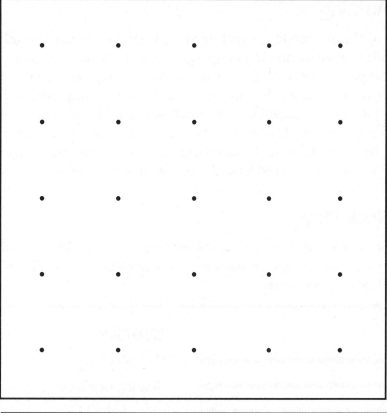

Name: _____ Date: _____

More About Math Centers

Math in the Morning

Even though most of the afternoon is spent in Math Centers, students should also have access to the permanent Math Center during the language arts time in the morning. Blocks should be considered part of the permanent Math Center during the morning center time. This includes small blocks such as interlocking logs, interlocking bricks, and a variety of plastic and wooden blocks to be used on the floor or tabletop. In addition to the small blocks there should be a classroom set of hardwood blocks. This is absolutely essential for kindergarten students and also provides a good learning experience for older children. More capable students can be encouraged to record the design of their favorite block constructions and keep those drawings in a classroom idea book.

Imaginative Block Play

An understanding of measurement and spatial relationships develops automatically when children play with blocks, but imaginations can also be stretched. Try to coordinate block building with the classroom theme. Here are some ideas:

Theme	Blocks
Dinosaur Play	Dino Zoo
Water	Boating or Fishing
Space	City on the Moon
Community	Block Furniture, House Plans
Maps	Hansel and Gretel Go Home
Native Americans	Village
Mexico	Mayan or Aztec Temples
Nursery Rhymes	Humpty Dumpty's Wall
Farm and Food	Barns and Pastures
Literature	Land of the Wild Things; Green Eggs Land
Fantasy	Wonderland
Holidays	Santa's Workshop
Transportation	Airport
Magic	Castle
Imagination	Color Land
Nature	Nature Museum
Family	Dream House
Animal Classification	Zoo
School or Friends	Playground
Patriotism	Lincoln's Home

More About Math Centers (cont.)

Math Manipulatives

The Math Center should contain a variety of store-bought and teacher-made math games and activities. The manipulatives listed below are to be used during the morning block, as well as for problem solving, operations, and number concepts during the afternoon math session. See pages 102–105 for additional lists of suggested materials to use in specific Math Centers.

- Pattern blocks and pattern block activity cards
- Animal counters (teddy bears) and activity cards
- Attribute blocks
- Sorting materials
- Nesting blocks
- Dominoes and dice
- Seriated rods or other rods
- Interlocking cubes with pattern cards and 100 grids
- Flannel board and felt shapes for counting and stories
- Links
- Math games, teacher- and commercially-made
- Addition and subtraction flash cards
- Counting cards, 1–20
- Buttons, rocks, beans, and other counting materials
- Clothespins with numerals written on them
- Various blank cards, scraps, and prepared materials for creating

Using the Math Center

The quick math lesson should be used to demonstrate the use of manipulatives and games as often as possible. Frequent modeling is necessary, or the children will simply use the materials to play house. This does not mean that the students should not be allowed to use the manipulatives in an imaginative way. It means that the children should get the most out of their play experiences in the Math Center. You can help by suggesting games and activities to try in an enthusiastic manner. If you feel that the children are not using the materials in an effective manner, try asking some questions about the play activity. Sometimes the usefulness of a mathematical or imaginative activity may not be immediately apparent to the observer, but careful questioning may reveal it. Use a friendly, inquisitive manner when asking students to talk about what they are making. Carefully worded suggestions can lead to problem solving. Example:

> *I see you are putting plastic bears in all the juice cans. I wonder how many bears are in this can? Do you think this can has the same number of bears as the other can? Can we match the bears from this can with the bears from the other can? I wonder how many inch cubes we can put in this can?*

More About Math Centers (cont.)

Planning for Center-Based Math

The biggest problem in planning a center-based math program is accumulating enough materials and storing them. During the morning, the classroom is set up in some or all of the following centers: library, dramatic play, themes, listening, research, art, publishing, and home. Just one area is designated as mathematics. **During the afternoon math block all the centers can be converted to Math and Science Centers.** This task requires careful planning and mobile math materials.

Suggested Math Centers

These are not etched in stone and may take different forms to suit the age levels and individual needs of each classroom. Feel free to use the centers that meet your students' needs and change the ones that do not.

Suggested afternoon Math Centers are number concepts, geometry, science and measurement, operations, problem solving, applications, creativity, and math research. Computers can usually be part of either the Problem Solving Center or the Math Research Center, or both.

- **Number Concepts** — This is often set up in the Block Center. Materials include:
  - Counting cubes
  - Related counting cube activities, i.e. laminated 1 to 100 charts, 100 board
  - Buttons
  - Numeral cards
  - Rocks for counting
  - Plastic teddy bears or other animal counters
  - Clothespins with numerals written on them
  - Commercial counting games
  - Commercial fraction manipulatives and related games
  - Plastic links and activity cards
  - Teacher-made number dot cards
  - Craft sticks or tongue depressors (for counting)
  - Teacher-made containers with numerals

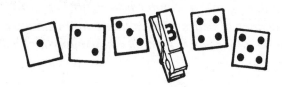

More About Math Centers (cont.)

- Measurement - This is often set up in the Theme Center for science. Materials include:

  - Large working clock model; small clocks for students
  - Clock stamp
  - Pictures of activities symbolizing different times of day
  - Tapes and books about telling time
  - Coin stamps (heads and tails)
  - Blank booklets for money and time activities
  - Tape measure
  - Scales, two kinds
  - Interlocking cubes
  - Plastic measuring cups and spoons; empty plastic containers
  - Rulers, yardsticks, metersticks

- **Problem Solving** — This can be set up in the Math Center. Some of the areas covered include: classifying and sorting, patterning, graphing, word problems, and creating problems. See pages 107-109 for problem solving activities. Materials include:

  - Dominoes
  - Paper scraps
  - Graph paper
  - Empty, transparent plastic containers
  - Blank calendars and sheets of numerals
  - Nesting blocks
  - Pattern blocks and activity cards

- Materials for sorting: lids, nature objects, toys, shells, plastic shapes, paper, sorting grids, counting sticks, plastic animals, plastic beans

  - Attribute blocks
  - Sentence strips
  - Blank word cards

- **Geometry** — These activities are often set up in the Block Center. Materials include:

  - Blocks
  - Linking cubes
  - Plastic or wood tangrams
  - Shape templates/stencils
  - Attribute blocks or other plastic shapes of various colors
  - Geometric models of a cube, sphere, cone, cylinder, rectangular prism, and triangular prism
  - Geoboards and rubber bands
  - Parquetry

More About Math Centers (cont.)

- **Applications** — This center is an attempt to replicate real life mathematics in a classroom center. Is it usually set up in the Home/Dramatic Play Center of the classroom. Many of the real-life play areas will need play money. Ideas for play areas that involve math include:

  - Restaurant with menus, order pads, and cash register grocery store with tags, labels, scales, play food, etc.
  - Space center or rocket ship (This could be adjacent to the computer area.)
  - Toy store with tags and items to make and sell
  - Home kitchen with no-cook recipes and measuring supplies
  - Art store, selling creations made by the students or parents
  - Table games and activities

Children can create their own areas of mathematics application, using their imaginations or experiences from literature. Get them started by creating a restaurant or store. After a month or two solicit additional center ideas from students. Let them create and stock the Home/Dramatic Play Center accordingly.

- **Creativity** — These activities are open-ended math projects that can take place in the Art/Publishing Center. It is possible that you might need to change the location of this center from month to month. If a large group sign up for this center, two or more centers might be used.

There should be no limits on the type of math activity done in this center. Students may design any type of project that shows something they have learned in math. This can be done on a large sheet of paper, in a math journal, or as the construction of a product. Emphasis is on recording for all except kindergarten students. Students are allowed to leave this center for a brief amount of time in order to borrow math books from the Research Center. Materials include:

- Flannel board with felt shapes
- Felt animals, vehicles, fruit, etc., for counting and sorting
- Magnetic counting and shape figures
- Art supplies
- Colored construction paper and scraps
- Story boards
- Trash bins with cardboard tubes, colored wire, boxes, etc.
- Art supplies
- Chalkboard
- Tape recorder
- Pre-cut pattern block paper shapes
- Geoboards
- Game-making materials (tablet backs, tag board, cardboard, etc.)

More About Math Centers (cont.)

- **Operations** — These materials are placed in one or more of the following areas: the Multi-Purpose Table, the Small Group Instructional Area, or the Reading/Skills Center. Materials include:

  - Calculators
  - Interlocking cubes
  - Story boards (made by students or teachers)
  - Flannel boards or carpet samples
  - Felt figures: shapes, butterflies, zoo animals (theme related)
  - Empty plastic bowls
  - Regular paper; large stiff paper
  - Pre-cut paper shapes
  - Paper number lines
  - Graph paper
  - Dice with dots
  - Dice with numerals
  - Game spinners
  - Blank teacher- or student-made books
  - Commercial addition and subtraction flash cards
  - Manipulatives: buttons, rocks, animal counters, shells, addition, and subtraction games

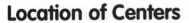

Location of Centers

The location of the centers should be decided by what works best for each teacher. Centers do not have to remain in the same place all year. They can also be combined or used for only part of the year. For example, it is unlikely that children will want to spend an entire year doing measurement. Locate the Measurement Center in the Theme Center for science, and the possibilities are endless. Measurement and math are always part of science in the real world. Placing math and science together provides a chance to call attention to and strengthen the math-science connection, which is essential to the future of a technological society. If the Science Center and the Theme Center are in the same location, you can plan many theme-related math activities.

More About Math Centers (cont.)

The Math Center as a Central Resource

Only one large Math Center stays set up all day, morning and afternoon. All the other Math Centers are temporary, to be used during the afternoon only. The large Math Center can serve as a resource for several centers. It can provide materials for three afternoon Math Centers: (1) Problem Solving, (2) Number Concepts and Geometry, and (3) Operations. Students working in the number concepts and geometry section can simply walk a short distance to obtain materials, such as counting games and geoboards. Some geometry materials can be permanently located in the Block Center to cut down on the amount of traffic. Most materials in the Math Center should be placed in baskets or other containers to make them as portable as possible. Another alternative is to place a small portable math shelf containing most of the geometry materials on top of the large math shelf and orientate it toward the Block Center. One special shelf in the Math Center could house counting games to be shared with the Number Center. It may be possible to place the manipulatives and cards for the Operations Center on a shelf near the operations table. Operations materials might also be stored in a basket in a closet. If that is not possible, students from the Operations Center could borrow materials from the large math shelf since it contains several sets of manipulatives.

Storing Math Materials

Math materials not used during the language arts block may need to be kept in baskets or plastic boxes in a closet or cabinet. Children will get bored if they interact with the same materials all day. Closed storage areas, such as cardboard drawers, may be kept out on shelves and declared off-limits during part of the day. Commercial math kits may be placed on top of shelves and declared closed until Math Center time. Planning for the storage of materials in the temporary Math Centers is one of the most challenging aspects of trying to set up a center-based mathematics program. Teachers who try to do it all at once may become frustrated and give up. Another common problem is trying to set up a room full of Math Centers without enough materials. Set up one or two centers at first, especially if materials are limited. Give some students a pencil-paper small group activity to do while the others work in centers. Small successes will build your confidence and help you feel enthusiastic about center-based instruction.

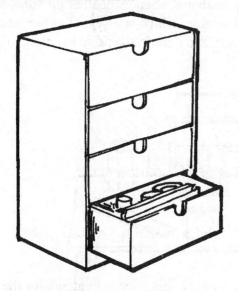
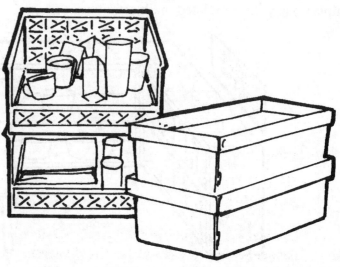

Problem Solving in Math Centers

Problem Solving — Level One

- **Sizes**

    Manuel was helping his mother put away some clean laundry. He was making two piles, one for his father's socks and one for his socks. How could Manuel decide which socks to put in each pile?

    Use felt cutouts on the flannel board or real socks in the Home/Dramatic Play Center. Have students verbalize what they are doing by asking: What are we doing? *(Sorting by size)*

- **Colors**

    Mother bought Jane some small baskets for her little toys. She bought a red basket, a blue basket, and a yellow basket. What color toys do you think Jane will put in the red basket? When you put red with red, what is that called? *(Sorting by color, classifying)* What will she put in the other baskets?

    Use real toys and baskets or use felt rectangles and toy cutouts on the flannel board. Follow up by sorting buttons onto cardboard cards by color.

- **Shapes**

    Ask the students to name things that are circles.

    Have them draw pictures and present their answers. Possible answers include:

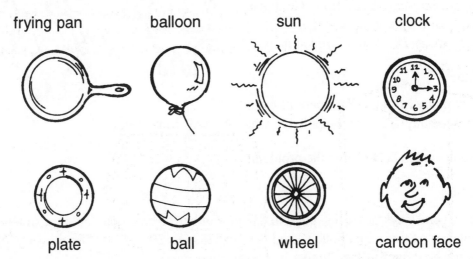

frying pan   balloon   sun   clock

plate   ball   wheel   cartoon face

- **Seriation**

    The school photographer told the teacher to line up the children in order by sizes. He said to start with the shortest and end with the tallest. How can he do that?

    Use real children in the math group. Dolls also work well, or make special cutouts for the flannel board. (See also Choosing Materials on page 67.)

Problem Solving in Math Centers (cont.)

Problem Solving — Level Two

- **Graphs**

    Show how many children bring their lunches each day and how many get a tray in the cafeteria. What is the best way to do that?

    Explore different suggestions for several days. Try different kinds of charts and/or bar graphs and markers. Children might draw their solutions.

- **Reasoning**

    Lawanda wanted to draw a picture, but she could not find her crayons. She asked her father if she could use some of his things to make a picture. Lawanda found something in her father's desk that she could use to make a picture. What do you think it was?

    Accept any reasonable answer. You may wish to have students look in your desk for ideas.

- **Reasoning**

    In the story of *The Three Little Pigs*, how many pigs do you think there were?

    As you show pictures from the book, call students' attention to the fact that there were three little pigs and one big pig, who was the mother. This is a good opportunity to use addition. Continue this lesson by asking how many cats there are in *The Three Little Kittens*.

- **Calendar**

    How many Mondays are there in April?
    On what day did April begin? On what day will May begin?

    Use the calendar to solve the problems.

- **Estimating**

    For several days or weeks, put a different number of bear counters in a small, clear plastic container. Start with about 10 and then increase to 20 and 30. If necessary, place the bears in a large container as the number increases.

    Explain to students that they are going to guess how many bears are in the jar. Point out that smart guess is called an *estimate*. After all students write down their estimates on the chalkboard or scraps of paper, invite a student to lead the class in counting the bears. When this activity seems to be getting easier, switch the objects to beans, buttons, counting cubes, pegs, crayons, marbles, macaroni, or any other materials from the Math Center.

Problem Solving in Math Centers (cont.)

Problem Solving — Level Three

- **Calendar**

How many days do we come to school in the month of April?

Give each child several calendar sheets to color or mark and try several different strategies. Provide a large calendar model at the front of the classroom. Even though the calendar is visible, do not mention this. Problem solving is about discovery.

- **Making Models**

Aunt Esther and Uncle Joe are planning a party. They need to borrow some card tables to have enough places for everyone to eat. They want everyone to eat in the living room. There will be 12 people at the party, counting Uncle Joe and Aunt Esther. How many card tables will they need?

Pass out cardboard squares, construction paper, and bear counters. Tell the children to make a model that shows how to solve the problem.

- **Making a Record of Discovery**

On the chalkboard, write this equation: 5 = 5. Discuss what *equal* means and how both sides of the equation have to have the same number. Then write 5 = 5 + 0 and show the corresponding domino.

$$5 + 0 = 5$$

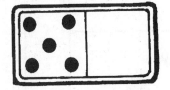

Place a set of dominoes on the table and ask the children if they can discover other "backward equations" like this? Have them write the equation and draw the domino for each. The next day write the reverse equations: 5 + 0 = 5, etc.

     #468 How to Manage Your Multi-Age Classroom

Domino Patterns

Glue the domino patterns onto stiff cardboard. Allow the glue to dry. Then laminate and cut out your dominoes.

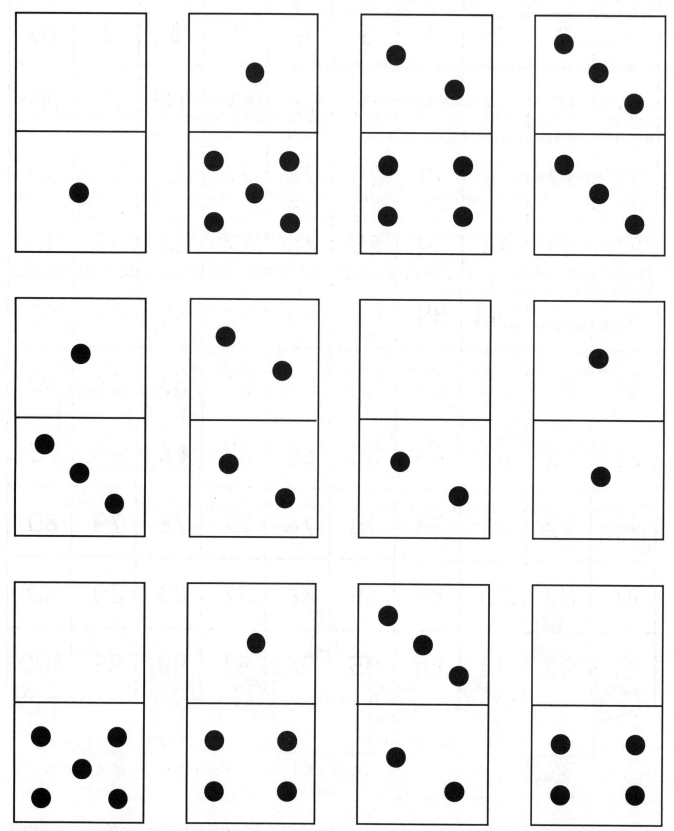

100 Practice Chart

Name: _____   Date: _____

1	2	3	4	5	6	7	8	9	10
11	12	13	14	15	16	17	18	19	20
21	22	23	24	25	26	27	28	29	30
31	32	33	34	35	36	37	38	39	40
41	42	243	44	45	46	47	48	49	50
51	52	53	54	55	56	57	58	59	60
61	62	63	64	65	66	67	68	69	70
71	72	73	74	75	76	77	78	79	80
81	82	83	84	85	86	87	88	89	90
91	92	93	94	95	96	97	98	99	100

Learn to count to 100. Touch each numeral as you count aloud. Then learn to write to 100. Copy the numerals from 1 to 100 until you learn to write them without looking at this practice chart.

Learn to Write to 100

Name: _____ Date: _____

❑ Practice Copy   Practice writing your numerals by copying the chart on page 111.

❑ Evaluation Copy   Write your numerals from 1 to 100 without looking at the practice chart.

Inch Graph Paper for Projects

Cut into strips and squares for open-ended math projects, such as graphs, number stairs, arrays, and operations.

The Importance of the Flannel Board

Benefits of a Flannel Board

In the primary multi-age classroom, there should be a flannel board available for all children to use, no matter what their ages. Older children benefit from literature-based play just as much as younger children. Children enjoy hearing a story that is read aloud, but the story becomes part of those children when they are involved with it through play. Learning to love books and use play to creatively extend literature experiences is critical to achieving literacy. It is always important to step back and look at the overall picture. What types of students are teachers trying to create? The end product of education should be imaginative students who love to read, can solve problems, and can think for themselves. Notice how closely these goals are tied to play. Making up stories on the flannel board is an imaginative, creative process that brings students closer to a love of literature.

How to Use a Flannel Board

Ideally students should hear the story during shared reading or read-aloud time. Then they should have the opportunity to create an activity that extends the story. They may simply retell the story, or they may use the felt figures of the characters to create new stories. The materials needed are the felt characters and props from the story, a flannel board, and a copy of the book. Some teachers are overwhelmed when presented with the task of creating and sorting felt characters from every book. Start with a few favorite books and break the task down into easy, manageable steps. Feel free to be creative.

Assemble Materials

Buy felt squares or felt pieces of many different colors. Then buy a large package of very tiny plastic eyes. Select a glue especially designed to make craft figures. Be sure that it will work well on cloth and plastic. In addition, you will need some very sharp scissors. It is often possible to make a pattern by tracing the outline of a character onto paper. Then cut it out and pin it to the felt for cutting. Some common character patterns are provided for you on pages, 116–119.

Plan Ahead

A little organization will save you time and energy. Look for stories that overlap so that characters can be in several stories. For example, an old man and an old woman can be used for Wanda Gag's *Millions of Cats* (Putnam, 1956) and also for *The Gingerbread Man*. Add a hat and the old man can become Old MacDonald. A set of farm animals can be used for the song and then chase the Gingerbread Man. Make three pigs instead of one, and you have the beginnings of *The Three Little Pigs*. The wolf that ate the pigs can also be the same wolf that tried to grab *Little Red Riding Hood*. The old woman from *Millions of Cats* can be Little Red Riding Hood's grandmother. The brick house built by the hard working pig could serve as grandma's house or the home of the Three Bears. Goldilocks can be Red Riding Hood by adding a cape and hood.

The Importance of the Flannel Board (cont.)

Flannel Board Pieces

Instead of making five or six different packs to match each story and trying to keep them sorted, place all the fairy tale flannel board pieces together in a plastic tote. Provide an illustrated list on the cover or inside the tote. Include a generic boy, girl, man, and woman. It is possible to make all of the Three Bears from the same pattern by enlarging or reducing it on a photocopier. This is also true of the Three Billy Goats Gruff. Add a few generic shapes like rectangles for tables, stoves, chairs, and beds, and semicircles for dishes. Listed below are a few ideas.

*Little Red Riding Hood**	Optional:
*The Three Little Pigs**	*Old MacDonald Had a Farm**
*The Three Billy Goats Gruff**	*Millions of Cats* by Wanda Gag (Putnam, 1956)
*Goldilocks and the Three Bears**	*Feel free to select any of the versions that are
*The Gingerbread Man**	available.

Model the Activity

If the felt pieces are simply placed in a center, it is doubtful that the students will use them in an imaginative way. Use the figures to present different stories, and students will mimic you. If you want them to make up new stories, you must demonstrate this activity also. Make up a story about how the Three Billy Goats Gruff went to visit the Three Bears and ate up all their sheets and curtains. Let the Gingerbread Man run from story to story while all the characters try to eat him. Be sure to point out how the same felt pieces can play different characters.

Add Other Packs

Later in the year add other large packs of felt figures as you have time. Be sure to enlist the help of parents. Here are some ideas.

Fantasy Pack — A family with crowns, castle, unicorn, giant

Christmas Pack — Santa, reindeer, elves, toys, trees, presents

World Pack — Asians, Hispanics, Native Americans, etc.

African Pack — Characters from Faith Ringgold's *Tar Beach* (Crown Publishers, 1991), African village, African animals

Space Pack — Astronauts, shuttles, rockets, planets, geometric shapes for buildings on planets

Math Pack — Small geometric shapes for geometry and counting; can also be used for Space Pack

Location of the Flannel Board

A flannel board can serve as an extension activity in almost any center. Since puppets and furniture fill the Home/Dramatic Play Center, it might be best to locate the flannel board in the Theme Center. It can also work well in the following centers: Reading/Skills, Art/Publishing, Research, or Listening/Author. A second flannel board is a good addition to the Math Center.

The Fairy Tale Pack

Goldilocks or
Little Red
Riding Hood

Big Bad Wolf

Cats

Ax

Woodcutter

Old Woman

116

The Fairy Tale Pack (cont.)

Gingerbread
Person

Bear
(make 3)

Pig
(make 3)

Goat
(make 3)

House

The Fairy Tale Pack (cont.)

Woman

Old Man

Troll

Bridge

118

The Fairy Tale Pack (cont.)

Fox

Hut

Turkey

Chick

Cow

Computers in the Classroom

Primary Students on the Computer

Students should be familiar with computers so they can feel comfortable using them. Children need to hear basic computer vocabulary which includes: computer, hardware, keyboard, mouse, monitor, screen, hard drive, disk drive, diskette, CD–ROM, software, program, cursor, space bar, enter/return, arrow keys, insert, delete, open, save, and print. Prepare several short lessons on computer care and operation. The next step is running an assortment of educational programs. The simplest ones move forward by pressing the space bar or enter/return key. Answers are indicated by moving the cursor with the arrow keys. Most educational programs used by schools reinforce concepts that have already been taught and help students learn to feel comfortable with computers. However, most experts agree that this is only part of what primary students need to learn with computers. Most computer time should be spent on programming and word processing.

Word Processing for Primary Children

Several companies make excellent programs that can be used to teach keyboarding skills. Although keyboarding is not required for young children, it is a definite plus. As with all skills, some students will be ready to learn how to type before others. Therefore, primary students must be allowed to progress at their own rate.

Allowing students to use a word-processing program on the computer is extremely important. This is because the children can learn reading and writing skills in a manner that is most likely to integrate them into our changing technological world. At an early age they can learn to compose and record their thoughts. Today's newspapers and magazines are filled with stories about authors who compose on typewriters and then transfer their work to word processors and others who are still writing in longhand on legal pads. Great care must be taken so that schools do not accidentally produce students who feel phobic about using computers or word processors. At an early age, children should begin to write using computers and continue to do so on a regular basis. In the future, no adult should have to go through technology shock while on the job. Word-processing instruction should begin at the kindergarten level, if not before, and continue throughout the primary grades. This is not a difficult task since young children can easily learn word processing when given the appropriate instruction and frequent access to computers. It is often easier for five- and six-year-olds to use a keyboard for composition than it is for them to use pencil and paper. You may find that compositions created on the computer are longer and more sophisticated than those produced by traditional methods. This is because some children lack the fine motor skills for good handwriting until they are seven or eight years old. In addition, using a computer can help decrease a student's fear of failure since the text can be revised and edited without having to rewrite the entire composition.

Software

CD-ROMs and Diskettes

Most new computers use CD-ROMs in addition to diskettes. CD-ROMs can store an enormous amount of information. For example, an entire encyclopedia can be stored on just one CD. Computers with CD-ROMs have full-motion video capabilities with sound and text. Many also offer a range of multimedia capabilities that allow users to create their own productions. Eventually most computers used in schools will have CD-ROM capabilities, making the others obsolete. However, because of the tremendous cost involved, it will take schools quite some time to update or replace the computers and software they are currently using. It is not unusual to walk into a classroom and see three different types of computers, such as an IBM, an Apple IIa and third brand of computer with a CD-ROM. All of these computers run different software. Because of Apple's emphasis on education, there was a large amount of educational software written on diskettes for Apple II computers. However, these machines have been considered obsolete for some time. As a result, many software companies no longer create new programs for the Apple II, and eventually they will quit selling the programs that are now available. One company that is continuing to create programs for Apple II computers is MECC. In addition to this line of software, MECC has other excellent programs available for the newer computers.

Suggested Software

MECC
6160 Summit Drive North
Minneapolis, Minnesota 55430-4003

Title	System Requirements	Level
Counting Critters	Apple 64K	PreK–K
First-Letter Fun	Apple 64K	PreK–K
Sum Stories	Apple 128K	K–2
Paint with Words	Apple 64K	PreK–2
Storybook Weaver Deluxe	CD-ROM for MAC and Windows	1–6
USA Geography	MAC; CD-ROM for MAC	1–7

The Learning Company
545 Middlefield Road
Menlo Park, California 94025

Title	System Requirements	Level
Reader Rabbit 1	MAC; CD-ROM for MAC and Windows	K–1
Reader Rabbit 2	MAC; CD-ROM for MAC and Windows	1–3

Software (cont.)

Broderbund
P.O. Box 6125
Novato, California 94948-6125
Phone: 1-800-457-4509

Title	System Requirements	Level	Other Information
Living Books • Berenstain Bears Get in a Fight • Just Grandma and Me • Little Monster at School • Harry and the Haunted House • Arthur's Birthday • Arthur's Teacher Trouble • The Tortoise and the Hare • The New Kid on the Block • ABC by Dr. Seuss	CD-ROM for MAC and Multimedia PC	Ages 3-8 Ages 3-8 Ages 3-8 Ages 3-8 Ages 6-10 Ages 6-10 Ages 3-8 Ages 6-10 Ages 3-7	Interactive screens; full-motion animation scenes; storybooks; games; teaching guides; songs
Math Workshop	CD-ROM for MAC and Windows	Ages 6-12	
Where in the World Is Carmen Sandiego? Junior Detective Edition	CD-ROM for MAC and Multimedia PC	Ages 4-8	Features clues and problem solving; requires no reading

National Geographic Educational Services
P.O. Box 98018
Washington, D.C. 20090-8018
Phone: 1-800-368-2728

Title	System Requirements	Level	Other Information
National Geographic's Wonders of Learning • Exploring the Solar System and Beyond • People Behind the Holidays • The Human Body • Our Earth • A World of Animals • A World of Plants • Animals and How They Grow • Seasons • Mammals: A Multimedia Encyclopedia	CD-ROM for MAC and Windows	Primary	Narrated texts; music; special ESL feature

Software (cont.)

IBM (K–12 Education)
Call for catalogues, product information, and location of the nearest dealer: 1-800-426-4338

Title	System Requirements	Level	Other Information
Write Along	Audio units; Printer; IBM or Compatible; Network and stand-alone versions available on disks and CD-ROM	K–2	Word processing; graphics; text-to-speech audio feedback for editing; draw editor for illustrations
Writing to Read 2000	IBM or Compatible; Network and stand-alone versions available on disks and CD-ROM	K–1	Features clues and problem solving; requires no reading

Sunburst
101 Castleton Street
Pleasantville, New York 10570-0100
Phone: 1-800-321-7511

Title	System Requirements	Level	Other Information
Muppet Slate	Apple II (128 K);graphics printer recommended	K–3	Word and picture processing program
Number Connections	MAC (2 MB)	K–3	Real problem solving; emphasizes process; has a word-processor
Balancing Bear	MAC, Apple II, IBM or Compatible, Tandy 100	K–3	Real-life and imaginary problems
Hop to It!	MAC, Apple II	K–3	Number lines; multiple solutions
A to Zap	CD-ROM for MAC or Windows	K–3	Letters, numbers, words
The Pond	MAC, Apple II, IBM or Compatible	K–3	Identifying and describing patterns

This company wins awards for its products and is often mentioned by its users. There are several products worth investigating. Sunburst offers a 45-day trial period.

There is also a special record-keeping system for teachers to record observations and assessments as they walk around the classroom, using an Apple Newton. It is called Learner Profile. This software is also available for MAC (4 MB + virtual memory) and Windows 3.1 (4 MB).

Changes in Assessment

What Is Happening?

In many schools a quiet revolution in assessment is taking place. Grade books are being replaced by portfolios and demonstrations of student achievement. Some schools have abandoned report cards completely. These are being replaced with anecdotal records and other evaluations. Letter and numerical grades do not always give enough information about the specific talents and needs of each child. Quite often test makers evaluate skills that are easy to test but do not reveal what the child has actually learned how to do. For example, it is possible for a gifted emergent reader to earn a mediocre grade on the phonics portion of a national achievement test even though that the child is already reading. Portfolio assessment addresses this oversight by allowing teachers to use observation to determine what the child can read. Then a list of the books the child has successfully completed is retained in the portfolio. Even a child's earliest attempts at writing and art can be preserved and documented in a portfolio.

Enhancing Self-Esteem

For students performing below the grade-level norm, report cards reflect only a series of failures. No wonder some children try to throw them away. Authentic assessment and/or portfolio assessment can be a means to show what these students can do, rather than what they cannot do. Because of the way statistics work, you must remember that no matter what happens in education, half of a nation's students will fall below the national average. Even if all children had the intelligence to be considered brilliant students, half of them would still be labeled as below average. This does not indicate a problem with students but, rather, the system used to evaluate them. This type of grading emphasizes deficits instead of showing strengths.

New Teaching Methods

Many of the new teaching methods are making the old ways of grading obsolete. Even the term *grading* is narrow and implies an absolute. A child is a growing and incredibly complex being. With portfolio assessment there is an emphasis on growth and detail. In the multi-age classroom every child in the room may be reading a different book. The teacher cannot give an end-of-unit test to the reading group. The teacher of the next grade will not know what books the child has read by looking at a letter grade. Nor do letter grades indicate a child's creativity, special talents, or critical thinking skills. The use of computers in the classroom also make traditional grading somewhat inappropriate. How does a letter or number grade answer questions such as:

> *Can the child use the computer to learn independently?*
>
> *What has the child composed using a word-processing program?*
>
> *How has the child's interest in computers and technology helped her/him learn other skills and gain information about other topics?*

With this in mind, take a first step toward portfolio assessment by reading pages 125-130.

Portfolio Assessment

How to Begin

Start collecting student work. Students can place completed work in a long flat box near your desk. The lid from a box of copier paper works well for this purpose. Some work will not be needed for the portfolio files and can be sent home immediately. Keep projects and papers that catch your attention. If you have ever saved work for Open House or Back-to-School Night, you will know how to select work for the portfolio. Place selected work in a box or cardboard "hot file" until it can be filed. It is absolutely essential to date all the work placed in the portfolio. A self-inking date stamp is ideal for this. In most cases just the month and year are sufficient. (Example: Jan. 96) Do not save any worksheets unless they represent a unit evaluation or a mastery check. Evaluations can often be made in a manner that will give more information than photocopied tests. If the file fills up with daily worksheets, it is time to expand your teaching repertoire to include some alternatives to workbooks and worksheets. Examining the work in the student files provides a quick self-evaluation of teaching methods, as well as student evaluation. The collected work tells parents and administrators a great deal about the student and the teacher.

Filing the Work

Put hanging files in a lower drawer of your file cabinet. Hanging files hold more work and are easier for children to use than standard file folders. Use a lower drawer so students can reach it and because it will enable you to do some work on the portfolios while seated. Label each file with a student's name, writing the last name first. Place the files in alphabetical order. You will need to collect more work just before an Open House, conference, or portfolio examination which is sometimes called a portfolio party.

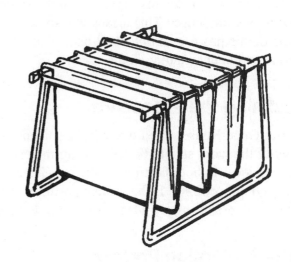

Portfolio Organization

A student assistant can help with the filing and organization of the work. The helper checks all the papers to make sure they have a date, either written by students or stamped by the teacher. You can also assign the job of stamping the date on the papers to a mature student. Next the helper checks to make sure the folders are in alphabetical order. An alphabetical listing of all the students' names can be written on a chart and placed nearby to assist beginners. Then this student neatly files the work. All papers without names should be returned to you.

The Collection Portfolio

The collection portfolio is a rough collection of all the work you have saved. It provides the material for the two more formal portfolios you will create for each student. For the collection portfolio, just toss in everything that looks interesting, in addition to all evaluations, pre-tests, projects, artwork, and unit tests. From this file, students will help you assemble two new portfolios: the student portfolio and the evaluation portfolio. Both of these are described on page 126.

Portfolio Assessment (cont.)

Building Portfolios

A week or two before the first Open House, begin sorting and discussing the work in the collection portfolios. Have a whole-class planning session to help students decide what to keep for their portfolios and what to take home. In many cases, photocopying their work will enable them to do both. There is a list of ideas to help you with the student planning process on pages 127-129. Students may forget to keep certain work from important categories, but you can guide them by making suggestions.

Student Portfolio

The student portfolio is the work that the student selects to show to his/her parents during Open House. Later this work may be shown to other interested parties such as administrators, other students, and, sometimes, other teachers. There is always the possibility the student might move to a new school, and this portfolio would make an excellent introduction. Even if the student is scheduled to return to the same class next year, it will be a good reminder to both teacher and child of the previous year's work. Although the choices rest mainly with the student, the assembling of the student portfolio is also a learning experience. This means that some students will need more guidance than others, making your role in this process an important one. This portfolio is intended to be displayed and should help build pride and understanding in the student.

Refining the Procedure

After Open House, weed through the student portfolio and send home some of the work. Determine if any of the work should be retained for the evaluation portfolio. If there is a need to have some of the same pieces in both portfolios, photocopies can be made. Continue to collect new work from the collection portfolio. If the student portfolio seems thin, try to assign more open-ended projects. Be sure to stress creativity when making these assignments.

The Evaluation Portfolio

In some schools the evaluation portfolio has taken the place of grade books. It contains documentation and is sometimes called an *assessment portfolio*. The evaluation portfolio is prepared by the teacher with the help of the student. It contains records kept by the teacher. These can include: conference notes, checklists, anecdotal records, tests, and work selected from the student's portfolio. There should be examples of the student's best work to substantiate grades on report cards, assuming that your school is still using them. For example, if one of the skills on the report card is sums to ten, there should be a test and/or project in the evaluation folder that shows how the student did in this area during that grading period. Copies of reading logs and reading records may appear in both evaluation portfolios and student portfolios. Sometimes the evaluation portfolio is used to help determine placement in special education or in gifted programs. The evaluation portfolio remains at the school.

Portfolio Assessment (cont.)

What Administrators Want in Evaluation Portfolios

1. Administrators want work from different subject areas: reading, math, writing, and possibly art, science, and social studies.

2. Collected work should show progress so it should be collected at the beginning, middle, and end of the year.

3. Confusing projects should be labeled so that everyone can determine what they are seeing. For example, the work of young children learning about patterns in math class should be labeled "patterns." If possible, more detail could be indicated like: "creating patterns" or "completing patterns."

4. The contents of each portfolio should be examined regularly. Then some of the work can be removed so that the portfolio does not contain more material than any human being could ever review. Remember that all of these portfolios have to be stored somewhere.

5. Administrators appreciate a description of the contents to show that organization and thought went into the creation of the portfolio.

6. Both administrators, parents, and other teachers want information as complete and succinct as possible. Do not include a long string of number or letter grades to show what a student understands about subtraction. It would be better to include an anecdotal notation that gives precise information.

    Example: May 95 — Bobby can do simple subtraction problems that do not involve renaming (carrying). He understands subtraction as take away but not as a comparison of two numbers. (Then include one subtraction test, a paragraph in which Bobby explains subtraction, and an open-ended math project.)

    Example: May 95 — Bobby created and wrote some subtraction problems.

7. Document as much as possible at the first of the year and/or at the beginning of a unit to show growth.

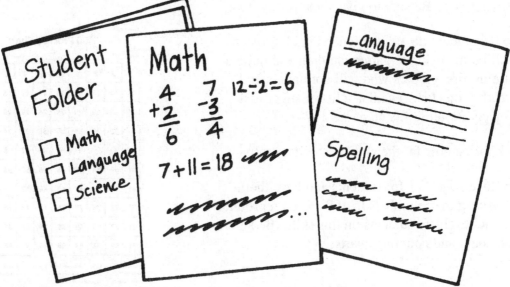

Portfolio Assessment (cont.)

How to Begin the Year

You probably already have experience with portfolio assessment, but you may not be calling it by that name. Each year, do you give some kind of beginning-of-the-year test? Do you have a checklist or some other instrument that helps you to understand the level of your entering students? To begin your evaluation portfolio, simply put these things in it. Up until now pretests were probably put in the permanent record file. If you are still required to do this, make photocopies for your evaluation files.

Documentation Suggestions

1. Have the child draw a picture of himself and date it. Also try to save a nice piece of art work that the child has created using tempera paint or watercolors.

2. Save the first entry in the child's journal. Older children can write a paragraph and illustrate it. Students entering first grade can write all the words they know how to spell and/or draw a picture. Kindergartners can write all the letters they know and/or draw a picture. If you do not wish to damage the journals by tearing out the first entries, make photocopies. For children in the pre-writing stage, be sure to get some drawings and take dictation about them.

3. Obtain a handwriting sample. Tell students to use their best handwriting to write their first and last names. Older children can add middle names, addresses, and phone numbers, too. Then have each child copy a list of words from the chalkboard. Have older children compose a short paragraph about who is in their families. Also have each student write the alphabet. Make a notation about whether the alphabet was copied or written from memory.

4. Give a math test appropriate to the student's level. Cover as many aspects of mathematics as possible. It may be necessary to give several small tests over a period of days so that the child does not feel overwhelmed. Be sure to give some review first.

5. Have the student do an open-ended math project. There will be many kindergarten children and quite a few returning first graders who will not understand what a math project is. There is a list of suggested math projects for all levels on pages 107–109.

6. Check to see how far the child can count orally.

7. Reproduce page 111 for students and have them practice writing their numbers to 100. Then reproduce page 112 and evaluate students on this skill. Be sure to cover calendars and counting charts.

Using Centers   *Math Centers*

100 Practice Chart

Name: _____ Date: _____

1	2	3	4	5	6	7	8	9	10
11	12	13	14	15	16	17	18	19	20
21	22	23	24	25	26	27	28	29	30
31	32	33	34	35	36	37	38	39	40
41	42	243	44	45	46	47	48	49	50
51	52	53	54	55	56	57	58	59	60
61	62	63	64	65	66	67	68	69	70
71	72	73	74	75	76	77	78	79	80
81	82	83	84	85	86	87	88	89	90
91	92	93	94	95	96	97	98	99	100

Learn to count to 100. Touch each numeral as you count aloud. Then learn to write to 100. Copy the numerals from 1 to 100 until you learn to write them without looking at this practice chart.

Portfolio Assessment (cont.)

Establishing a Reading Baseline During the First Six Weeks

1. Have the student read to you from the last book listed on his/her reading log. Use the Reading Record (page 48) to write observations along with the title, author, and date. Note whether the child uses context, first letter with context, picture cues, self-correction, sounding out words, etc. Then ask him/her to read from an unfamiliar book that is at an appropriate reading level.

Reading Record

Student's Name: _____

Date	Title and Author	Observations

2. Textbooks and other materials from the formal reading program are useful in determining the student's current reading ability. Since everything is rigidly determined as to grade level, text materials are very useful for evaluations. Check the teacher's guide (especially the appendices) for formal and informal reading tests and checklists. Use these as pre-tests.

3. Take an inventory of sight word recognition. You may wish to use a prepared inventory for this purpose or create one of your own. This is suitable for all second graders and some first graders. An inventory of pre-reading skills would usually be more appropriate for kindergartners, as would a letter recognition test. Do not assume first graders know the names and sounds of the letters; be sure to test them on these skills.

Use a Writing Checklist

During the first six weeks record writing observations, using a writing checklist. Evaluate punctuation and capitalization as well as structure.

Ask the students to compose at the computer using a word-processing program. Save several samples early in the year. If the student wishes to take them home, make copies of them for the portfolio. Compositions that students generate on the computer are excellent evaluation tools. Make every effort to save one or more each six weeks to show growth and skill application.

Authentic Assessment

Authentic assessment has always been in existence. Every time teachers show children's work to parents or administrators, they are using authentic assessment. The only thing that has changed is the emphasis. Teachers and schools are moving away from letter and number grades toward actual examples of student work. Examples of student work show more than what has been passed or failed. They show areas of strength and weakness. A more indepth analysis is possible when the specific skill is shown in context. It is also much easier to perceive growth. Many abilities, such as organization or imagination, are readily recognized but would be invisible in a system of reporting that only allows for letter or number grades. Teachers who keep notebooks to demonstrate student work have always been using authentic assessment. Now there is an increasing effort to share these notebooks with parents, administrators, and students themselves. Authentic assessment must represent what the student has been learning.

Portfolio Chart

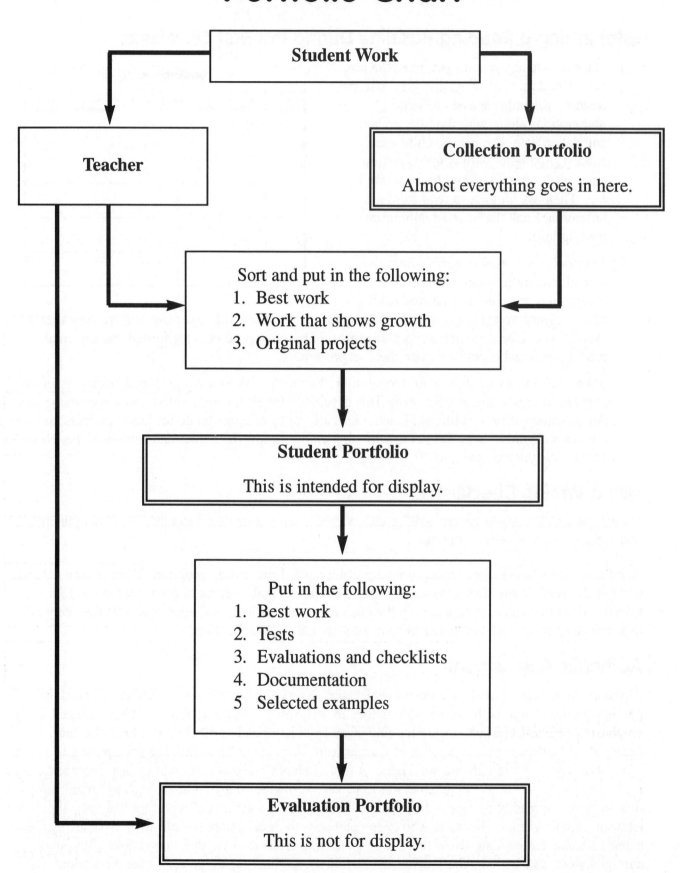

Student Work

Teacher

Collection Portfolio

Almost everything goes in here.

Sort and put in the following:
1. Best work
2. Work that shows growth
3. Original projects

Student Portfolio

This is intended for display.

Put in the following:
1. Best work
2. Tests
3. Evaluations and checklists
4. Documentation
5 Selected examples

Evaluation Portfolio

This is not for display.

Taking Anecdotal Notes

Using Anecdotal Records

Anecdotal notes are not a new method of record keeping. What is changing is the way anecdotal records are being used. Until recently, the most common method of reporting to parents was the use of letter or numerical grades. Today, there is more emphasis on anecdotal records and checklists. The reason is that anecdotal notes offer more specific and useful information than grades. They also invite more parent participation. As parents become more aware of the specific strengths and weaknesses of their children as students, they will become more and more involved with their education.

How to Keep Anecdotal Records

You may need training and practice to keep good anecdotal records. The easiest way to begin is to pretend to be a video camera. A video camera records everything and makes no judgment. It is very accurate. Be as specific as possible. Here are some examples:

Poor: Johnny is a good reader.

Better: Johnny is reading with speed and fluency. He often chooses reading as an elective activity.

Poor: Betty is very shy.

Better: Betty is very quiet in class.

Poor: Andre is struggling with math.

Better: Andre is continuing to work on addition facts with sums of 5 or less.

Poor: Norma is a good math student.

Better: Norma has learned how to count by 5s and to count backwards.

Poor: Judy is a sweet little girl.

Better: Judy follows class rules.

Poor: Brian is all boy.

Better: Brian has an occasional infraction of class rules.

Avoiding Problems

It is best not to write negative comments about students. They could alienate parents and cause problems. Sometimes it can be difficult to report accurately to parents without offending them. At the same time, you need to give a clear picture of the child's progress. No matter what type of student is begin evaluated, try to be as objective as possible. Do not compare one student with other students. During a conference, be sure to compare the student's work with her/his previous work. Quantitative reports are also very effective in anecdotal reports. Example: This is a list of the books your child has read this year.

Parent-Teacher Conference Form

Student's Name: _____ Date: _____

Teacher: _____

Points to Discuss

Strengths	Weaknesses

Conclusions/Goals:

Parent Comments:

Signature of Parent: _____

Skills Assessment

Student's Name: _____

Subject: _____ **Grading Period:**_____

Skill:	
Skill:	
Skill:	
Skill:	

Preparing for a Substitute Teacher

Lesson Plans

There is some question whether lesson plans are still necessary in their old form. The most compelling argument for lesson plans is that they are necessary for the substitute teacher. Actually a substitute folder is probably more help to the sub than the standard lesson plans. Here is a sampling of some of the things to include in the substitute folder.

1. Copies of the daily schedule — Include two copies: a brief form to glance at quickly and a more elaborate form with explanations and special directions. It may also be necessary to make a special physical education, music, and art schedule.

2. Class roll

3. Forms for lunch and attendance, with a sample of each already filled out

4. An explanation of your record-keeping procedures

5. Sheet with the morning jobs explained — Make a copy of page 23, Beginning the Day, and put it in the folder. There may be other pages in this book that you will want to copy and place in the sub folder.

6. List of children leaving for special classes — Provide the child's name, the type of class (speech, special education, etc.), and the time.

7. Class rules and discipline procedures

8. Worksheets for reading, math, and a morning sheet — The sub can use the morning worksheet to put students to work after the morning jobs. Although worksheets are no longer used as much as they once were, they remain an excellent choice for the substitute.

9. Big Book suggestions — If there is a Big Book that you have been meaning to read, place it near or on your desk. Then put the accompanying idea book in the sub folder.

10. Dismissal procedures — Clearly explain all dismissal procedures. Make a chart that shows the names of car riders, walkers, bike riders, and bus riders. For the students who ride buses be sure that section of the chart includes bus numbers.

George	Daryl	Isacc	Gary
Mike	Renee	Charles	Martin
Beverly	Kim	Bob	Jacob
Diane	Ron	Sharon	Sally

11. Provide access to a VCR and movies — Describe exactly how to obtain a VCR. Tell the location of movies at your school and the procedure for checking them out. Provide a list of suggested movie titles that you feel will extend a theme that students have been studying.

Preparing for a Substitute Teacher (cont.)

Can a Substitute Handle a Multi-Age Classroom?

There is no question that the job of the substitute in the multi-age classroom is more difficult than the traditional graded classroom. Most substitutes will not be familiar with the multi-age setting and may be apprehensive. It is strongly suggested that the district require a training session for substitutes. You may need to suggest that your educational service center offer this type of training opportunity.

A sub hired for a week or less may actually find that the multi-age classroom is easier to manage. The students are usually involved in self-selected activities as they work in centers. During a short teacher absence, the substitute does not attempt to do the guided lesson for small groups. Instead she/he circulates from center to center, observing work and maintaining discipline. Emphasis is placed on presentation of products and correct clean-up procedure. The sub may wish to shorten center time and allot more time to reading aloud or doing worksheets. Movies are always a good choice for the afternoons. Students can usually benefit from repeated viewings of educational films. *Swinging Safari* (National Geographic, 1994) and related wildlife videos make excellent choices. Science topics, such as dinosaurs and ecology, are always good choices. There are also many excellent videos of classics literature available. For example, there is the video *Linnea in Monet's Garden* (First Run Features, 1994), a movie that was based on an outstanding piece of literature. There is an entire series of excellent books entitled *Reading Rainbow Series* (Great Plains National Instructional Television Library) available on video. This series consists of both fiction and nonfiction selections, and each includes a commentary or lesson.

Some other wonderful movies include stories by Dr. Seuss and a large number of Golden Book videos. Build a personal film library by using bonus points from book club orders. Having your own videos enables you to closely coordinate teaching units with related films. It also means they will be readily available in case you have a sub. It will be helpful to the sub if you provide suggestions of films that can be used for review or to extend the theme being studied.

Lesson Plans

Since there is seldom one lesson for everyone in the multi-age classroom, the concept of lesson plans needs to be revised. There are many ways to do this. You may wish to design your own plans to include features that best suit the needs of your students. It is usually helpful to experiment with several different formats. Keep your plans as simple as possible to eliminate unnecessary paper work. Complicated is not better, just more time consuming. Designing an efficient new lesson plan should be a priority since once an individual or school establishes a format, it is often hard to make a change.

Examining Your Day

Make an abbreviated daily schedule, using the form on page 137. Perhaps there are a few things that involve the whole group each day. Some of these will only need a time indicated on the plans. Other activities will require listing a title or an activity description. Here is one example:

Name: Ms. Jones   Date: January 5

Theme: *(Indicate the name of the theme, i.e., pets.)*

Morning Duties: *(Provide a description of any preparation that must take place before students arrive, i.e., making the Science Center into a veterinary hospital.)*

Attendance/Lunch Helper: *(Write the student's name.)*

Time	**Activity**
(Indicate the starting and ending times of each activity on the right side of the chart.)	Shared Reading *(Tell the name of the book the skill to be emphasized and any extra materials, such as dolls or flannel board figures, to be shown. Tell where the extra materials should be placed after the shared reading.)*
	Quick Lesson: *(Tell the skill to be covered for this lesson.)*
	Sustained Silent Reading
	Reading Groups: *(Name the books and page numbers to be read by each group. If the book is to be the group's choice, indicate that as well.)*
	Centers
	Presentations
	Recess/Lunch
	Read Aloud *(Indicate the title of the book and pages to read.)*
	P.E./Music/Art: *(Give the time and place.)*
	Quick Math Lesson: *(Name the skill and describe the activity.)*
	Math Centers: *(List special topics.)*
	Math Presentations/Summary
	Homework: *(Describe the assignment.)*
	Dismissal

Lesson Plans (cont.)

Name: _____ Date: _____

Theme: _____

Morning Duties: _____

Attendance/Lunch Helper: _____

Write the time and name of each activity in the chart shown below.

Time	Activity

Behavior Management

Better Discipline

Begin by teaching a few quick lessons on discipline. Since small groups do not meet during the first four to six weeks, this time can be spent teaching students about your behavior management plan. The students need to be trained to work effectively in centers. In the past, children sat in desks and did their work without interacting with each other, although some creative teachers had centers for children to use when they finished their work. There is some similarity in the multi-age classroom. Children do their silent reading followed by reading response, but no effort is made to give them worksheets so that they will stay in their seats. When reading response is completed, they go to megacenters and spend long blocks of time there.

How Behavior Is Managed

1. Discipline is controlled by student choice. Children behave better when they have choices. Students can choose their centers during sign-up time. Once in the center, several activities are available to keep them interested and busy. They are free to create and design their own projects. There is usually no assigned work in the centers. Sometimes students do not complete work during small groups and are allowed to finish in centers. Such projects are not usually worksheets. They are more likely to be things like literary map making, designing games, or writing plays. Several elements are essential to the success of this system. Students must be trained to know what type of behavior is expected. Do not assume they know what to do. Remind them often during the trouble-shooting speech each morning. At the beginning of the year, limit their choices. As children gain experience and maturity, add more choices. Do not put out all the center activities at first. Gradually add manipulatives.

2. Behavior is controlled by freedom. This may sound like a contradiction, but it is not. Children behave better when they are free to act like children. They must be able to talk and play with each other during centers. Forcing adult standards of behavior on children results in rebellion. This does not mean that there are no standards of behavior, just that children are expected to act like children. We hope they will be well-behaved children. Freedom in a classroom has limits. Except for an occasional outburst of giggling, singing, or drama, noise must be somewhat controlled. How loud should it be? This question can only be answered by the individual teacher. When the noise level is disturbing you, it is too loud. Normal conversation should be possible. The arrangement of the room should separate loud and quiet centers. If students are trying to read aloud at a teacher table, they should not be located next to the Home/Dramatic Play Center, Listening Center, or Science Center.

Behavior Management (cont.)

Grouping Helps Control Behavior

Design your grouping at the beginning of the year. You may find out immediately that heterogeneous groups behave better than groups in which all children are the same age and ability level. Mixing age and ability within groups cuts down on competition and promotes cooperation. Older students can model behavior for less mature ones. Grouping requires constant adjustment and varies with every class. Some classes will learn to group themselves in centers and other activities with little teacher supervision or interference, while others may require many suggestions and changes before they are allowed much freedom. There will be some students who have trouble controlling their impulses, and these children should never be grouped together. Sometimes there may be several impulsive children in a single classroom. Keeping these children in separate groups and arranging the seating so they are not close to each other may be time consuming, but it will be worth the effort. These students can and should be taught to do this for themselves when signing up for centers. Instruct these students that they cannot sign up for a same center. Be very specific when telling an impulsive child the students he/she cannot be near.

Centers Help Control Behavior

There is less inappropriate behavior when students are working in centers. Student stress decreases when they do not have to sit quietly in desks, and the decrease in stress usually results in better behavior. Just letting the students spend time in centers may automatically improve discipline. However, behavior is never perfect, and sometimes problems arise. If this happens, use the suggestions provided below.

1. Be sure that individual students remember and understand the rules for centers.

2. Model many different projects and activities during quick lessons and small group lessons so that students will have plenty of ideas.

3. Appoint a center helper or center team to go around and check the centers each day to make sure all materials are properly put away at the end of the day.

4. Make note of any problems so that they may be discussed in damage control the next day.

5. If the entire room becomes too noisy, consider cutting center time short to let the children take a break. Keep work on hand that can be assigned to take up the extra time. Let students know that center time has been shortened because of excessive noise.

6. When there are persistent problems during centers, do an analysis of materials available. Boredom and misbehavior will result if there are not enough materials or the activities are not changed frequently enough. For example, the same puzzles should not be left in centers all year. Buy a few new puzzles each year so that there will be plenty of variety. Sometimes puzzles can be coordinated with themes. Some themes that usually have puzzles to match are fairy tales, dinosaurs, animals, ecology, transportation, space, and nursery rhymes.

Behavior Management (cont.)

Students Take Responsibility

Help students understand that responsible behavior leads to more choice, more freedom, and more time in centers. Students who do not choose a project to work on temporarily lose their right to choose. They must listen to a repeat of quick lessons about behavior and procedures or listen to an instructional tape on choosing a project. During this time period, assign work, and the student does not get to choose activities, work partners, or centers. Repeated infractions lead to more extended assigned work.

Procedures for Dealing with Disruptive Students

1. Remove the student or students from centers and have them sit in time out. Do not interrupt other activities to negotiate the dispute until a natural break occurs in the flow of activities. Students are usually not allowed to return to the center and might lose some recess time. Check district rules on required recess time before denying recess. If the student creates more than one or two disruptions, he/she should be assigned to a center with a different group next time.

2. Students who do not sit quietly in time out must sit next to you until lunch, dismissal, or another designated time.

3. Repeated offenses require a phone call to the parent.

4. Repeated phone calls require a trip to the office for an instructional lesson on behavior from the principal or assistant principal.

5. Repeated visits to the office require a conference with the parent. At this time, referral to the counselor, behavior specialist, or other appropriate intervention should be discussed.

6. Continued problems require detention time or more visits to the office for discipline.

7. At this point, you should meet with the principal and/or appropriate committee to determine future actions or referrals. Throughout the entire process, it is essential to keep good documentation and to carefully follow district policies. See the section on keeping anecdotal records (page 131). These can apply to documentation for discipline, as well.

Behavior Management (cont.)

Weekly Behavior

Monday — Date:	Tuesday — Date:

Wednesday — Date:	Thursday — Date:

Friday — Date:	List Consequences
	1. Name on board — 2. X by name — 3. XX by name — 4. XXX by name —

Questions, Questions, Questions

Why Have Multi-Age Classrooms?

Children learn at different rates. The rate of learning is not steady but proceeds in periods of rapid growth mixed with periods of little or no measurable growth. The system of first grade, second grade, third grade, etc., assumes that children learn at predictable rates, with all of them arriving at the same point at the same time. As a result, many children must repeat a grade, sometimes even kindergarten. The results are usually devastating. Children become stigmatized and lose self-esteem. Some children give up. Research shows that retention greatly increases the chances that students will drop out of school. Students who are retained twice have a drop out rate of 90%. In the book *The Non-Graded Elementary School,* John Goodlad and Robert Anderson (Teachers College, 1987) found only negative results from retention. More recent research by state education agencies all conclude that retention is harmful to children.

Another consequence is that rigid performance schedules are causing an increase in the numbers of children entering special education. Many of these children come from a home environment where learning is not encouraged during the first five years of a child's life. Often they are immature, as well. To expect these children to catch up with other children by the end of first grade is often unreasonable. Sometimes children can succeed if they are taught the basics when they are more mature. At this point, rapid instruction can sometimes help them close the learning gap. Multi-age classrooms are one way this problem is being addressed.

Are There Any Advantages for Average or Gifted Children in Multi-Age Classrooms?

Rigid performance schedules may be harming these children, as well. They also learn at individual rates and can become stressed or bored with the pace of instruction. Gifted children have the opportunity to work and play with older children. They are not bound by grade level limits on learning but can continue as far as they wish. Children become more like adults, expert in some areas and mediocre in others. Computers will destroy many traditional grade level boundaries, no matter what schools do.

The old system of reading groups and seat work caused children to spend most of the morning confined to desks, filling in blanks and answering questions in workbooks. Whole-language practices have improved this situation to a great degree. Master teachers have always found a way around practices that are harmful to children by individualizing instruction and using classroom learning stations. While it is not necessary to have a multi-age classroom in order to individualize instruction, it can be helpful because it forces a change in teaching methods. Teachers become teachers of children, instead of reading teachers and math teachers. The multi-age classroom is child friendly. Children are mobile, more responsible for themselves, and often happier. Anecdotal records made during observations also show that these children do better in future schoolwork, no matter what type of classroom they enter in later years.

Questions, Questions, Questions (cont.)

How Can I Find Time to Teach This Way?

Some teachers fall victim to planning and paperwork in their multi-age classrooms. A few confessed that they had little or no personal time left. The best way to avoid this situation is to do most of your creative tasks during class time as a demonstration for small groups. Students need to see the act of creation. Modeling is the best way to teach children how adults approach tasks. For example, if you wish to make a game about telling time, sometimes it is not necessary to assemble all the materials ahead of time. Think out loud in front of the group. If you are using an activity from a book, read the directions aloud. Question if the book's directions are the best way to accomplish your objective. Discuss whether changes need to be made. For example: What modifications are necessary to make the game more durable? What is the best way to present the game for use in the centers? How difficult should the game be? Ask the children for their ideas. Let them help you assemble the materials that are necessary. Make lists and write them on the chalkboard or chart tablet. If the activity takes more than a few minutes, write down a list of materials and continue the next day. Naturally, this activity is more suitable for seven- to nine-year-olds.

How Can I Get Everything Done?

Let your students help you do things. Most teacher-made activities require some coloring. Make it a rule never to color anything yourself. Let students outline with markers and then color with crayons. If they realize that they are assisting a teacher, they will work very carefully. Nevertheless, be prepared to accept some less-than-perfect results. Errors can sometimes be colored over or glued over before laminating. Materials will look like they have been made by children, and that is good. Sometimes things will have to be thrown away, and it will be necessary to start over. Children need to understand that these things happen to adults, too. If mistakes are handled tactfully, students will learn to take risks. Before doing any task yourself, ask if it can be successfully completed by a student under your direction.

Are There Any Other Ways to Save Time?

Getting organized will help save you time. Try not to stuff everything into a drawer. Prepare a teacher work box. A plastic box with a handle is excellent for this purpose. Put in a set of washable markers, a package of crayons, scissors, glue, tape, black permanent markers with broad and fine tips, rubber magnetic strips, felt, and tacky glue. Place the box on a shelf behind your desk within easy reach. Next to the box, stack pieces of stiff cardboard like those found on the backs of writing tablets. Also, arrange a stack of colored index cards on the other side of the box.

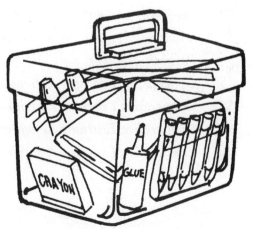

Both the gray tablet backs and the colored index cards can be purchased from printing companies. If you wish to work at home, prepare a duplicate box. Students can be very helpful when creating classroom materials. Supervising students in their creative efforts is not a waste of time. To involve students in making materials for the classroom, assemble some work boxes for student use.

Professional Reading and Resources

Baratta-Lorton, Mary. *Mathematics Their Way.* Addison-Wesley, 1993.

Chase, Penelle, and Doan, Jane. *Full Circle, A New Look at Multi-Age Education.* Heinemann, 1994.

Cutting, Brian. *Getting Started in Whole Language.* The Wright Group, 1989.

Davis, Rodney. *The Nongraded Primary...Making Schools Fit Children.* American Association of School Administrators, Arlington, Virginia, 1992.

Goodlad, John, and Anderson, Robert. *The Non-Graded Elementary School.* Teachers College, 1987.

Kovacs, Deborah, and Preller, James. *Meet the Authors and Illustrators.* Scholastic, Inc., 1991.

Lipson, Eden Ross. *The New York Times Parent's Guide to the Best Books for Children.* Random House, 1988.

Montessori, Maria. *The Montessori Method.* Schocken Books, 1964.

Richardson, Kathy. *Developing Number Concepts Using Unifix Cubes.* Addison-Wesley, 1984.

Routman, Regie. *Transitions.* Rigby & Heinemann, 1988.

Teacher Created Materials, Inc.

059 *Learning Centers Through the Year for Primary Classrooms*

144 *How to Manage Your Whole Language Classroom*

145 *Portfolio Assessment for Your Whole Language Classroom*

188 *Using Math Manipulatives for Cooperative Problem Solving: Bear Counters*

197 *Science in a Bag*

198 *Social Studies in a Bag*

199 *Math in a Bag*

342 *Connecting Math and Literature*

343 *Connecting Geography and Literature*

344 *Connecting Writing and Literature*

345 *Connecting Social Studies and Literature*

346 *Connecting Art and Literature*

373 *Thematic Bibliography*

504 *Portfolios and Other Assessments*

517 *Managing Technology in the Classroom*

546 *Portfolio Planner*

650 *Cooperative Learning Activities for Language Arts*

653 *Cooperative Learning Activities for Social Studies*

656 *Cooperative Learning Activities for Math*

659 *Cooperative Learning Activities for Science*